THE SACRED Journey

God's Relentless Pursuit
of Our Affection

BRIAN & CANDICE SIMMONS

BroadStreet
P U B L I S H I N G

THE SACRED  Journey
God's Relentless Pursuit of Our Affection

By Brian & Candice Simmons

Published by BroadStreet Publishing Group, LLC
Racine, Wisconsin, USA
www.broadstreetpublishing.com

Cover and interior design by Chris Garborg at www.garborgdesign.com
Interior typesetting by Katherine Lloyd at www.TheDESKonline.com

Printed in the United States of America

15/9–1

CONTENTS

INTRODUCTION

Come with us on the sacred journey—a wonderful, mysterious journey into the passionate heart of Jesus Christ. Incompressible in its fullness, we will walk together through a devotional study of the Song of all Songs. You are about to be touched by the greatest prophetic song ever composed. It is not simply the greatest song of Solomon's, but it is the greatest song of all songs. Solomon wrote 1,005 songs (1 Kings 4:32), but nothing can compare to this masterpiece of divine love.

Inspired by the Holy Spirit, the lyrics of this song are written to change and transform your very being. Jesus Christ will be revealed as the heavenly Bridegroom, the love of God made Man. You will see Jesus as the refiner and His love as the flame—making us into pure gold that reflects His glory and His passions.

We discover in this song the power of affirming words that are spoken into our destiny. Many will tell you what is wrong with your life, but only Jesus brings you words of love when you feel you are at your worst. Your guilty accusations are drowned out by His words of endearment. Every chapter will overflow with truths that make you wonder if they're simply too good to be true.

But first, it is important to grasp the story line of the Song of Songs. It is much more than a book of erotica, as so many have limited its meaning, reducing it to a manual for sexual pleasure in the context of marriage. However, the greatest pleasure of all is walking in intimacy and tenderness with Jesus Christ. He brings a sweeter song with greater pleasures than anything we can ever experience in this life. His pleasures delight the human spirit and fill our hearts with bliss.

You are the one who is loved by Jesus in this story. Be careful not to miss that and assume the lyrics of this love song are for someone else, somehow excluding you. You are the Shulamite, while Jesus is the King. The Hebrew root word for *Solomon* and the Hebrew root word for *Shulamite* is one and the same word—one is masculine while the other is feminine. When you believe and follow Jesus, you are one with Him, for the one who joins himself to Jesus is one spirit with Him (1 Cor. 6:17).

Within the pages of *The Sacred Journey* lies the heartbeat of Jesus Christ. His passion, His jealous love, His longing to make you completely His—these are the noble themes of this story. Embrace it as your own today. Jesus wants to share His life and His throne with you. But the preparation to make you fit for a King is surprisingly unique. He prepares His bride by convincing her of His love for her, even in her weakness. You will find no angry exhortation here, and no exasperation at her failures. He doesn't shame you into maturity, but loves you into the fullness of your destiny. He puts a crown upon your head and watches you grow up to fit it.

How to Interpret the Song of Songs

There are at least three basic schools of thought for interpreting the meaning of Solomon's greatest song. God is so complex and fascinating that He has embedded in this divine allegory multiple meanings. Perhaps each could be considered as valid and helpful for our lives. But I believe the greatest way to interpret it lies in our relationship with the heavenly Bridegroom, Jesus Christ. Nevertheless, let's take a brief look at each of these three schools of thought.

1. The Natural Interpretation (Validating Human Sexuality)

Those who adhere to this approach view the Song of Songs as God's endorsement of our sexuality, especially as it relates to a husband and wife in the context of marriage. Although it is possible to glean some help through the metaphors and symbols of this interpretive model, it comes far short of reflecting the fullness of God's beauty within the Song of Songs.

Keep in mind that Solomon had multiple wives and concubines, affairs with women who were not his wife. To make Solomon's greatest song simply one of his many polygamous affairs is not a perfect model in which to interpret the Song of Songs. Indeed, if that is the true way to view his book, making human sexuality the highest song, the greatest song ever composed by the wisest man on earth, we are left wanting more.

The earliest records of church history reveal that the fathers of our faith wholeheartedly believed that the Song of Songs is in the middle of our Bible as a literary "Holy of Holies," with the highest theme found in all of God's Word. That highest theme is the story of divine romance, the sacred journey into the fiery passions of the love of God. Of course, God has created man and woman with sexual needs and desires, but He has also made us living spirits who are able to commune intimately with Him. That union and communion is a more fitting approach to viewing this parabolic masterpiece.

2. Jewish Historical Interpretation (Validating God's Love for Israel)

This school of thought interprets the Song of Songs as a powerful description of God as the Bridegroom and Israel as the one chosen and loved (Jer. 2:2; Hos. 2:16–20). To understand the layers of Solomon's greatest song requires that we pause and look deeply into God's heart for the people He has chosen—the people of Israel. However valid this model of interpretation is, it is limiting in scope to only Israel, thus missing the entire unfolding of revelation in the New Testament to the people of God. The God who "so loved the world" has given us treasures in every Old

Testament book that are meant for every believer today—God's all-encompassing love of Jew and Gentile has been expressed by the life, work, and Spirit of Christ.

3. The Allegorical Interpretation (Validating Jesus's Love for His Bride)

This figurative approach to interpreting the lyrics of Solomon's song requires the unveiling of our hearts and the unveiling of God's wisdom. To see in the symbols a higher reality, a glory tucked inside of metaphors and allegorical terms, will reveal the heart of Jesus Christ to us in ways never seen before.

Solomon was a king, but Jesus is a King greater than Solomon. The Shulamite fell in love with this King, not merely the earthly king who was named Solomon. Let the symbols and emblems disappear as you watch the reality of Christ's love for us manifest. Each phrase is a picture for us, full of color, vibrant truth, and poetic nuance. It is important that the story of our sacred journey unfold before us, to know and love the King of the universe in this way. This is the approach we have taken in unfolding the truths of divine romance in this book. We pray you will find the substance of Christ's unending love for you in each verse and on every page.

THE STORY HIDDEN IN THE SONG OF SONGS

So what is the story line and how does it impact our life? There is a story embedded within the story. It is a parable hidden inside a parable. It causes us to peer and ponder with a holy curiosity before it will yield its meaning.

The Holy Spirit wants to unfold this book to you as an allegory of Solomon and the Shulamite—how a king takes a "nobody" and makes her into the princess bride. Using deeply symbolic language, Solomon has composed this sacred journey to help every tenderhearted reader see the love of a greater king than Solomon, the love of God as seen in the life of our Lord Jesus Christ.

Love meets us at each step of the journey. We are tested, yet affirmed. Trials surround us, but so does His strong arms of love and compassion. The Shulamite fails Him, and so do we at times, but nothing can diminish the love of our Bridegroom for us—the love that keeps us and sustains us. It is the story of the ages—the greatest love story ever told and put into music with lyrics—that will change your concepts of God and His love for you. It is the story of the Shulamite and the King.

Jesus is the King of Glory who is first seen in the book as a kind Shepherd. You are the Shulamite, beloved follower of Jesus Christ, for you are the one He sings His song over each and every day. This may in fact be the song of the Lamb that will be heard in heaven, which is sung by a multitude of those who have conquered the "beast" of our old life (Rev. 15:3).

Along the way of the sacred journey, you will see the Shulamite surrounded by friends, known as the daughters of Zion. These are the brides-to-be, those not yet ready to enter into their own experience of flaming passion for Jesus, but they will one day. These ladies-in-waiting will, at the end of the Shulamite's journey, cry out for the "kiss" for themselves. This begins another cycle of loving devotees of Jesus.

The book ends where it begins, with another company of lovers who cry out for the "kiss" of His divine love. As they watch the tender love of the King for His beloved, they want it too.

We will also see in the plot of this divine drama the emergence of the "watchmen," or caretakers, which point to the spiritual overseers who have guided us, helped us in our personal journey, and led us deeper into God's ways. Sadly, there is an episode where the watchmen hurt the bride, wound her, and take away their covering from her. Spiritual jealousy always turns one against another.

So we encourage you to read *The Sacred Journey* as though you were overhearing a duet sung by you and your Lord Jesus right there in your home. These words will free your heart to live with tender first-love devotion to Him. Whether you are a man or a woman, young or old, you can see in this story a beautiful example of how your love will mature with bridal affection for the Son of God until one day its flames consume you.

We believe that a study of the Song of Songs has the potential to light a divine fire within your soul. The Holy Spirit is giving us glimpses of a higher realm for us to live in—the realm of divine romance. May you enter in and experience this sacred journey for yourself.

Brian and Candice Simmons

CHAPTER 1

THE KISS OF GOD

The Lord your God has arrived.
He's inside of you even now.
What wealth and mighty power he brings you—
saving you and giving you victory.
He will take such delight in you
that it will make him leap for joy, twirl and spin,
even shout with great gladness!
You will be his feast of joyful pleasure!
Yes, he will renew you with his love.

(Zephaniah 3:17)

Open your heart today as the Holy Spirit calls you to take a bold step into the sacred journey of His love and passion. This is the journey into the flaming heart of Jesus Christ, and it will lead you into the pathway of the Shulamite bride. Along the way you will be blessed and broken, filled with and knowing failure, cherished and challenged. Yet in the end you will be consumed with Him—His love and compassion and tender affection toward you.

The Lord is calling His people into the flames of divine romance. We are His bride, not just His worker bees. Our hearts must be stirred by every new glimpse we see of the love of Jesus.

Are you ready to come along on the journey of discovery of the flaming heart of God?

The most amazing song of all, by King Solomon. (1:1)

The Song of Songs is a divine opera, the most powerful piece of music ever written. It is a song written by King Solomon almost three thousand years ago—a song that tells an incredible story of love. It is incredible because it's yours. It has been included in the Bible to lead you into the flaming heart of Jesus Christ. Once you've heard the music, nothing else can make you dance. So the sacred journey begins with a cry from a passionate heart:

Smother me with kisses—your Spirit-kiss divine. (1:2)

This is what every heart cries out for—the divine kiss to consume their soul. The *"Spirit-kiss"* is a metaphor that speaks of sacred intimacy with Jesus Christ. The most powerful gift God can give to the human spirit is His kiss. Kisses from God impart the deepest longings that could ever be given to the human spirit. His divine kiss is the only answer of why we are here on the earth. It is what made Adam, the man of clay, into a living expression who was created in the image of God. Dust and deity mingled when the Maker kissed His Spirit-breath into Adam.

Your Creator knows that true transformation comes by a relationship—a powerful relationship with Christ where love's torrent covers your sin and makes you lovely in His sight. Jesus never comes to scare us into submission, but He woos us into intimate friendship with Him. God delivered His transforming truth and the grace for change in a *relational* package—the person of His Son. Grace has a face, and His face is smiling toward us each and every day.

Walls that keep us from intimacy must come down. We can no longer hide behind a wall of our ugly and demeaning feelings about ourselves. Jesus sees in us a suitable companion that will flood His heart with joy for all eternity. We need to fill our mind with the truth of how God sees us. Others will always judge us by our greatest weakness, but God sees the glory of His Son shining in us. Our hearts tell us we're not worthy: "I am a bad person in so many ways." But we need to remember this: the love of our King has stepped out of eternity. It is not a momentary thought or simply a mood God has at moments throughout history—it is eternally ours in Christ Jesus. Since His love is an eternal love, it will not end the first time we fail either. Since His love endures forever (Ps. 118:1), then we can enjoy all of it we can.

Smother me with kisses—your Spirit-kiss divine. (1:2)

There are places in your heart that will only be healed by divine romance. So run into Abba's arms today and abandon yourself completely to Him. If you could ask for anything in prayer today, *this* is what you should ask for: *"Smother me with kisses—your Spirit-kiss divine."* Notice the Shulamite doesn't ask for a sermon or for success or for Him to tell her how great she is. She doesn't ask for a reward or for information; and she doesn't even ask for a miracle. She simply wants to be kissed by the King.

Don't think of Jesus actually kissing you on the mouth when you read this; rather, think of God awakening your heart with His power and love. Think of God's Spirit falling on you with a fresh passion to know your Bridegroom-King. This kiss from the King is a metaphor of intimacy with Jesus, a heavenly kiss that awakens the human Spirit to His affections toward us. A Spirit-kiss comes to us each time we open our hearts to the Word of God and draw close to Jesus.

God does not wait until you are perfect before He enjoys you. In fact, He loves the weak, the immature, and those who feel incomplete. Think of Jesus placing a crown on your head and then watching you grow up until you fit into it. He calls you a hero before you ever act nobly. Today, Jesus smiles at the thought of you. He is the Lover of your soul. You really are His personality type, for He made you in His image. A kiss is one of the tenderest expressions of love known to humanity. Every person in the world can understand its meaning, regardless of gender, race, or culture. A kiss is the first thing we give to our newborn as he or she enters the world and the last thing we do with a loved one who is leaving this life. The longing for a kiss is deep in the heart of every human being. We all want the tender show of affection from others, but would Jesus love us that much? The words of His mouth are the superior pleasures of life. His heavenly kiss is not the joining of mouth to mouth, but the joining of God with humanity.

With God's friend Moses, God spoke *"face-to-face"* (Num. 12:8). But in the Hebrew language, it actually says that God spoke "mouth to mouth." God spoke to Moses "mouth-to-mouth." This is the kiss of His Word to our spirits. It is the longing of the soul to be united to the Word of God, to be touched by the heavenly.

The bondage of the church is about to be broken by a kiss of divine love. Divine romance will melt away the distance and fear that has hindered His bride for so long. We cry out to Abba and say, "Let Your Son, the Son of Your splendor, let *Him* kiss me with the kisses of His Word. Let Him kiss me with His kisses of affection, with His kisses of mercy, and with His kisses of forgiveness.

In the parable of the prodigal son (Luke 15:11–32), we find a father who ran to his wayward son when he returned, hugging his neck and kissing him. In the Greek text it is in a verb tense that suggests that he kept on kissing him, not just kissed him once. Aren't you glad that our Father loves the one who stayed and loves the one who strayed? Let the Lord kiss you over and over again until you can't take any more.

"Let Him *kiss me"*—not just His prophets. It must be the impartation of His words flowing from His mouth into mine (Ps. 119:131). I don't need a messenger or an angel, but Him. Not interpretations from His teachers, but the Word that comes from *His* mouth. *"Let Him kiss me"*—the one beloved of His Father, kissed by His Father. When the Father kisses the Son, it imparts

the depths of infinite love, transcending anything known on earth. When the Son kisses me, His complete love fills me with a knowledge and depth of revelation that can't be fathomed. When the Son of God kisses me with the Word of God, I am changed forever, never to be the same again.

Furthermore, *"let Him kiss* me.*"* I have watched the wonderful way He loves others, but would He bring His kisses to me? I don't want others to tell me about His love, I want to experience it for myself.

**So kind are your caresses,
I drink them in like the sweetest wine! (1:2)**

The Shulamite's cry for kisses brought Him near. She prayed to the Father that the King would come with kisses. He appears before her and now she speaks to him directly: *"So kind are your caresses, I drink them in like the sweetest wine!"* The love of Jesus is the most pleasurable thing to the human heart. Nothing is more delightful. Nothing can compare to the caresses of His love.

There is a wordplay in the Hebrew here, similar to a pun. The word for "kisses" and the word for "take a drink (of wine)" is nearly the same word. The implication, as seen by ancient expositors, is that God's lovers will be inebriated with His love, by the intoxicating kisses of His mouth. Wine is a symbol of the pleasures of this world (Ps. 104:15). His better-than-wine love is more pleasurable than any blessing known on earth. The wine of this world cannot touch me like His love. The pleasures of His love are pure and clean. The joys of a thousand worlds cannot compare to the joy of being with Christ. If only people knew there was a sweeter, cooler fountain to drink from. It is far more refreshing than anything this world has to offer—this intoxicating love of Christ. Haven't you found His love delightful to the depths of your soul?

Drink in this love, drink deeply of the passions of His heart. Receive this mystery deep in your heart: God loves you in the same way that God loves His Son. The measure of the Father's love and affection for Jesus is the measure of Jesus's love for us: *"I love each of you with the same love that the Father loves me. Let my love nourish your hearts"* (John 15:9).

The love of the Father for His Son in all its intensity is the same love the Father has for you. This is the ultimate statement of your worth. Jesus left everything to make you His own. Can you drink in the sweetness of that thought? Unmerited love! He has loved you freely, without requiring anything in you to attract such love. He sought you, He bought you, and He brought you back to Himself. You can say to your Friend, *"So kind are your caresses, I drink them in like the sweetest wine."*

The Shulamite is seeing the absolute truth of this in her life. All is empty apart from Him. Eternal love has gripped her heart. She will no longer be led astray by the pleasures of an empty world. The divine kiss has caused her to forget all that is in the world. Fullness has overwhelmed her. She must know this love that is better than the wine of love that He pours out for her. Do you want to know this better-than-wine love?

> **Your presence releases a fragrance so pleasing—**
> **over and over poured out.**
> **For your lovely name is "Flowing Oil."**
> **No wonder the brides-to-be adore you. (1:3)**

When you truly understand the personality of Jesus Christ, then you will find Him to be like the most pleasing fragrance. The cologne of His compassion—what can compare to it? Can you smell His fragrance, sweeter than the rose? The fragrance of His presence is so pleasing, so winsome and inviting. It speaks of who He is, what He thinks, and what He feels. This is the fragrance of His beautiful personality—His internal qualities of love and gentleness will capture you, just like the Shulamite. She is swept off her feet, lost in the fragrance of God. She is beginning to understand the emotions of His heart.

Jesus's lovely personality is filled with passion for His people.

How pleasing He is to the troubled and tested ones. His personality is filled with loving desire. He evaluates our lives with such kindness. Because of who Jesus is, how He feels, and how He processes life, He sees loveliness in us. The Shulamite says that His presence releases

a fragrance so pleasing—over and over poured out. (1:3)

To smell His fragrance, you must be close to Him. The Shulamite has drawn near and is touched by His sweetness. She can tell by His countenance, by the look in His eyes, how much He enjoys her and longs to be with her. She has never seen such love expressed before. His smile beams with love. His thoughts of her are powerful yet kind. His invisible sweetness has touched her (Luke 7:47). Who would not want to sit at His feet and pour out on Him the adoration of worship?

The loving ways of Jesus are like the most pleasing perfume. We must no longer hold thoughts about God in our hearts that are not true. The key that unlocks the heart is to understand this wonderful and fragrant personality of Jesus. Can you feel the pleasure of His kiss? Can you taste His sweet wine? Can you smell the fragrance that is poured out from His presence?

Just saying His name is like opening the finest flask of costly oil. Jesus. His name touches us deeply. His character is revealed in that name. His name speaks of His works, His deeds, His character, and His leadership. Just to think of Him opens our hearts to the sweetness of true love. Jesus's deeds are lovely and wise, appearing as fragrant oils. The Shulamite is now realizing how wise and good He is with those who love Him. She cannot be offended with the one who is perfect in all His ways. He knows what is best, He does what is best, and He always works in wisdom. He is truly more desirable than any other.

For your lovely name is "Flowing Oil." (1:3)

The name of Jesus is oil in the Father's hand, and that oil is poured out over us. His is the only name the Father has poured forth. Poured out at Calvary. Poured out at Pentecost. Poured out on me and poured out on you.

When His name is poured out like oil or perfume, the lost become passionate lovers of God. The anointing for ministry is found in the poured out name of our Beloved. Mary of Bethany poured out the perfume of love on Jesus's feet until the fragrance filled the house. Healing is in His perfume, His lovely name. Our love covenant with Him gives us the right to use the power of His name to bless the nations. Say to your Beloved: "Let Your lovely name be poured out upon me, Lord Jesus!"

No wonder the brides-to-be adore you. (1:3)

This can also be translated as "how right they are to adore You!" Who are these "brides-to-be" who are following the Shulamite so closely? They are believers who have yet to be gripped with holy passion for the Son of God. They are sincere and true believers, but they are immature in their love. This entire story is the saga of how the brides-to-be, following the King from a distance and watching the way of a Man with a maiden, become Shulamites and begin their pursuit of the Bridegroom. The book will end where it begins…another Shulamite will arise and cry out for a kiss from the King.

No wonder we adore Him, for Jesus cherishes the immature and weak believers. We must have more songs to sing about His love. The world must know that Jesus is a friend to the sinful one. "Lord, no wonder our hearts swell at the mention of Your name! To see You is to love You. How worthy You are, Prince of Glory, to receive the love of all." This divine song will awaken you to pursue your divine Friend. Plead with Him to reveal more of His endless love to your heart, so that you may give it all back to Him.

No wonder the brides-to-be adore you. (1:3)

Jesus is everything that righteousness stands for. He is the perfect example of manhood, perfection, grace, and uprightness. Those who are upright in heart will see in Him their perfect model and spouse. How right it is to abandon our lives to Him. Do you adore Him? Are you passionate about Him?

Pray this prayer today: "Lord Jesus, I see now that You are infinitely kind—kinder than I have ever imagined You to be. Your willingness to walk with me and love me has completely changed me. I thank You for the changes I'm beginning to see in me while on this sacred journey. I want to know the power of Your love until I can love others with the same love You have for me. Amen."

CHAPTER 2

YOUR LIFE VISION

**Draw me into your heart and lead me out.
We will run away together into your
cloud-filled chamber. (1:4)**

The call of God burning in your heart today is more than just a desire to "do something" for God. It is the uncontainable, unstoppable passionate longing to meet with the Lover of your soul and hear His heartbeat for your life. Here is the prayer of awakened desire: "Draw me into your heart and lead me out." The Shulamite is asking to be drawn away in sacred intimacy with the King—drawn out of her comfort zone, drawn away from sin and self, into the loving arms of her Beloved.

Nothing else can satisfy the thirst she feels for her Lover. She is ready to make a break from everything else to follow Him alone. In spite of her weakness, she longs to be drawn to Him and to be taken away from all that is unclean and impure. She has tasted His Spirit-kiss and the fragrance of His anointing, but she longs to be drawn with even greater power and glory. Is this your cry today?

When we ask to be drawn after the Son of God, we are asking that He be exalted to the highest place in our hearts. The maiden recognizes that spiritual growth is a response to God's drawing love as it tugs at her heart. None of us seek God apart from His tender influence on our spirits (John 6:44), first drawing us toward Him. His touch draws us to His heart, as He longs for us to know Him as He truly is.

Do you have a longing to be close to Jesus today? He will draw you so close that it breaks every chain that holds you back, every weight that holds you down. Even if He has drawn you a thousand times in the past, ask Him to draw you again. Cultivate a friendship with Him. See yourself as His partner, His companion, the one He wants to be with. He will be more to you than you can ever think or imagine.

Jesus draws us into His chamber to groom us for our eternal inheritance. He will *"take us away"* from our self and ambitions so that we will run together with Him. Running with Jesus with all your heart is the only proper response when He draws you with His tender mercy and compassionate love. It is an act of holy zeal. To run after Him will eventually bring us into His arms. We will become holy partners, touching others with this love that flows from His heart. We are drawn into intimacy so that we will be His partners in ministry.

Passion for Jesus always results in compassion for others. Jesus is on a mission, and He wants to include you in that mission. He is changing the hearts of people with the power of His love. The Son of God is longing for a bridal partner, not just a girlfriend. He is looking for one who will run with Him to do the Father's business.

Running represents obedience in action. We must hurry to do His will—not with a striving heart, but resting at His side. We don't stop "running" the first time we get hurt or discouraged. We don't stop running when others fall at our side or when we are persecuted and misunderstood. This race we run is a destiny that is already sealed in our hearts. Nothing will stop us from running when we set our eyes on the Beloved and our hearts on pleasing Him.

Jesus will have a bridal partner at His side who will run with Him to touch the nations. As we sit at His feet long enough, we will be willing to get our feet "dirty" in serving this world. One day, if we will continue running with Jesus, our panting soul will find Him and He will bring us to His secret place, fully and ultimately.

We will run away together into your cloud-filled chamber. (1:4)

The King's chamber? Would Jesus really take *me* into the dwelling place of the King? This divine, celestial chamber room is where God carries us into special experiences of His grace. This is His secret, private chamber where He discloses Himself to the seeking heart; it is the treasure house of His heart. He does not bring us merely into the courtyard, but into His chamber, where we experience personal encounters with our King and fresh impartations of the Spirit in the secret place.

The Hebrew is actually "a chamber inside of a chamber," referring to the innermost chamber. This is where the King dwells, and this is where the King draws us. The Holy of Holies was actually a chamber inside of a chamber. This Holy Place is where Jesus wants to take you and me. We run into His heart and enter into His cloud-filled chamber. Only Jesus our King can bring us into the chamber room where He alone dwells. We enter not by our striving or maneuvering; He must bring us in by redeeming grace. Jesus is the Shepherd who carries the lamb over His shoulders, into His chamber (Luke 15:5). Still, we must pray and ask Him to take us in and reveal His glory to us.

Divine fellowship in His sacred chamber awaits us. There will be a banqueting table prepared in that place, but for now we must be alone with Him in His chamber room of intimacy. In this place we receive the living bread, the manna of His presence that nourishes our spirits.

The chamber of His heart is open to us. What sacred mysteries He reveals in His chamber! Do you hear His invitation? Do you see the open door (Rev. 4:1)? Can you trust Him to bring you in? Surely, one so holy, one so beautiful as He, would have better friends than us. Yet it is to us that this invitation is issued.

No longer reluctant or preoccupied, the maiden wants to be

where He is. "Take me into Your palace of glory; take me into Your chamber, Lord Jesus—where I can hear Your message of love." In His chamber He will share His secrets with us. Happy are those who are brought into that wonderful place of revelation and impartation.

Imagine what this King could reveal to you if you spent time in His chamber, where only trusted friends were allowed to enter, exchanging friendship with a King. Wisdom, knowledge, and all the riches of Christ may be found in the beautiful gallery of the King's chamber. The maiden cries out for kisses of intimacy and promises to run with Him. He responds by leading her into the chamber room experiences of deeper revelation.

Every one of us must have a secret history in God, a hidden life in His chamber. This is where the Lord develops us and matures us in preparation for running with Him. Jesus has gone to prepare a place for us, and that place is His chamber room full of power, revelation, and love. It is the hiding place prepared for you.

The King's chamber is open to every seeking heart, for it is in that place that He will share His secrets with you. You will taste the delights of sacred intimacy with the heavenly Bridegroom. Don't think you must wait until heaven to be drawn into His chamber. Ask Him to bring you in today. Search for the chamber of the King and you will find Him within the veil.

We will remember your love as we laugh and rejoice in you, celebrating your every kiss as better than wine. No wonder righteousness adores you! (1:4)

The daughters of Jerusalem overhear this outburst of passion and they too are drawn into the delight of this King. They are stirred by the passion of a seeking heart: *"We will remember your love as we laugh and rejoice in you."* Every believer will one day be drawn into the spiritual realization of ecstasies that excel anything known on earth. It is called *"inexpressible and glorious joy"* (1 Peter 1:8, NIV).

The one thing that will draw immature believers into pursuit of Jesus is a heart on fire. A "holy virus" is released when others see your undying love for the King. As you become His friend, others are excited about following Him in this way too. The daughters of Jerusalem are stirred to a new level of devotion and delight as they see the maiden drawn to the King. Rejoicing in God is the result of new levels of passion for Jesus (Phil. 3:3).

Celebrating your every kiss as better than wine. (1:4)

So many things could come between our Beloved and us—so many worldly sorrows and disappointments work to hinder us from rejoicing in His love. Our failures, our wandering hearts, our hard thoughts…yet we will celebrate *"your every kiss as better than wine."*

The Hebrew actually states, "We will *remember* your love more than wine." It is at the Lord's table that we build a memorial of love to the Son of the Father. We cannot forget this love that is greater than any other. Through the participation of the bread and wine, we draw near and are taken into the realm where symbols become substance.

There is a love we can praise every day of our lives—the love of the King. As we drink the cup of communion, we remember the intoxicating sweetness of His kiss of love that is better than the wine. The Shulamite resolves to make her "theology of love" more important than the pleasures of this life.

The Song of Solomon begins with the cry of the bride and her companions saying, *"We will celebrate your every kiss as better than wine."* She vows to remember His affections throughout her journey, and in her darkest nights she will remember to meditate on the kiss of His love He has revealed to her in times past. This is a beautiful and necessary vow she offers.

Yet it is only an echo of a greater promise, the promise of the Lord Himself. He says to our fainting hearts as we come to Him time and time again with our sometimes feeble prayers: "I will remember your love, My beloved one, for all eternity. I will reveal the relevance of all the weak moments of faith that you have long forgotten, and My Father who sees in secret will reward you openly. I will remember your love."

No wonder righteousness adores you! (1:4)

The Shulamite speaks this over her King while she is enthralled with His presence. He embodies all that is good and right: *"No wonder righteousness adores you!"* It is with good reason that every tender heart should adore Him.

Pray this prayer today as you take communion: "Jesus, I draw near to You in this moment with the bread and the cup. I feast on Your love and drink of Your tender mercies. You satisfy me as nothing else can. I celebrate the love You have for me that was seen as You bled on the cross to pay for my sins. No wonder You are loved for all eternity. I love You, Lord Jesus. Amen."

CHAPTER 3

HE CALLS US LOVELY

The Shulamite speaks:

**Jerusalem maidens, in this twilight darkness
I know I am so unworthy—so in need. (1:5)**

The Shepherd-King interrupts her and says:

Yet you are so lovely! (1:5)

Standing on the stage is the goat-keeping girl, the Shulamite. The blazing sun has beat down upon her for years. Her low self-esteem and the labors of life have taken their toll on her. But her cry for the chamber room has opened the door of her heart.

Brought into His chambers, the maiden discovers the darkness of her heart. She sees her sinful desires, even mixed motives hidden within. The deeper we go into the heart of Jesus, the more we confront our own weaknesses and shameful ways. It seems as though we get worse rather than better. This is God's way of preparing us for the next step in our sacred journey.

Passion for Jesus is the pathway into the heart of God. To fall in love with Jesus and to abandon our heart to Him is the noble threshold we must all cross on our journey into the heart of God.

But to love Him will cost us everything.

In the beginning, it seems like a fantasy that He would come and enjoy such sacred intimacy with one like me. But little do we know that loving Jesus will lead us not only into His heart, but also into a new revelation about our own condition. To know Jesus is to be emptied of self-confidence and selfish ambition. He will spare nothing to make us over again into that image of glory. But wait until you hear what He tells you in His chamber room.

In His chambers the maiden cries out, I'm *in this twilight darkness, I know I am so unworthy—so in need.*" Her heart is corrupt and she knows it. The word for *darkness* means scorched or darkened by the sun. Solomon says that life "under the sun" is vanity and will "scorch" our soul.

This is the first crisis in the Shulamite bride's journey—the revelation of her own sinfulness. Each one of us must face this truth: we have been marred as those of Adam's race, fallen into disgrace. But as she bows her head in the presence of His splendor, she hears Him say,

Yet you are so lovely! (1:5)

Could it be? Did He really call her lovely even when she felt so dark and sinful? Would Jesus call *me* lovely too? But doesn't He know my heart…my weak, weak heart? Yes, He knows all things, and still He calls *us* lovely, even in the midst of our weakness.

Place these two phrases together: *"In this twilight darkness, I know I am so unworthy—so in need,"* and, *"Yet you are so lovely!"* The cry of the awakened heart is: *"I know I am so unworthy—so in need!"* But when we are brought into the King's chambers and stand in His presence, we hear Him say, *"Yet you are so lovely!"* His love conquers fear, unbelief, and the shame of failure. The strong current of love in His eyes drowns rejection out. It is right and good for everyone to worship and adore the Son of God. We have tasted of His love. A deeper passion to know Him has gripped our hearts. Are you ready for more?

So what is it that makes us lovely to God? It could never be our performance, for we have failed over and over again. Rather, our loveliness is found in the image of Jesus and a willing spirit that longs for Him. He loves us even when we are darkened by sin, with wrong desires and still consumed with immature ways. He calls us lovely, because deep down we sincerely want to obey Jesus and know Him in fullness.

Abba's "anyway love" is here. He can say, "Yes, I know and you know that sin has brought shame, but *I love you anyway.* Your longings for Me make you lovely. With a willing spirit you will go on to a mature bridal love."

God has infinite passion to see you through the growth process. He will not leave you half done. He is the God who finishes what He begins (Phil. 1:6). Throughout life, every new chamber room experience will bring an even deeper understanding of unworthiness. You will cry out each time, "O, Lord, I am darkened by my sin." But if you listen carefully, you will also hear your King say, *"Yet you are so lovely!"** The voice she hears from the shadows whispers to her: "You may seem dark, but you are lovely to Me!" Imagine the King bringing you into His chamber, not to tell you what is wrong with you, but to tell you how lovely you are to Him.

The Shulamite speaks:

**I feel as dark and dry as the desert tents
of the wandering nomads. (1:5)**

The Shepherd-King responds:

**Yet you are so lovely—
like the fine linen tapestry hanging in the Holy Place. (1:5)**

The maiden sees herself as *"dark and dry as the desert tents of the wandering nomads."* ** These tents were made from animal

---

* The Hebrew word for *lovely* can also mean "graceful, loveable, and desirable."

** Literally, "dark as the tent curtains of Kedar." There is a wordplay in the Hebrew here, as the word *Kedar* means "a dark one" or "a dark place." This was the name of skins and were darkened by prolonged exposure to the sun. She again sees herself as a dark room with no light shining in, full of the works of the flesh. However, listen to the King of Glory describe her:

Yet you are so lovely—
like the fine linen tapestry hanging in the Holy Place. (1:5)

Solomon only used the finest of linen to make his tent curtains. He is saying to the Shulamite, "You see yourself dark and covered with shame, but let me tell you what I think of you. You are as lovely as the white tent curtains that I use in My dwellings. You are like the finest linen curtains in the Holy of Holies."

Only the priests could see the beauty of these curtains suspended in the sanctuary of the Most High. Only the living God knows your true worth, your true beauty. Outwardly, they see only the dark tents, but inwardly your Bridegroom sees white linen.* Others may delight in seeing your distress and darkness, but your Lover-Friend delights in seeing your inner beauty. He will look at you in your tomorrow and rejoice over you as one who found great treasure.

Your own righteousness may seem to be dim and dark like the tents of Kedar, but the King of Glory sees far beyond your failure to see your inner being, who you are at the core of your being. He sees your glistening spirit like a gleaming white linen curtain hanging in the sanctuary of the Holy Place. This is truly who we are in Christ.

Yet you are so lovely— (1:6)

Most people have struggled with how they see themselves. We often view ourselves as ugly, stupid, immature, and sinful. Yet in the midst of these confused emotions, we hear the voice of our Bridegroom speaking to us, *"You are so lovely."* He never exaggerates or distorts the truth. The Word of our Lord can be trusted.

---

one of the sons of Ishmael and represents our old Adam life.

* Fine linen in the Bible speaks of righteousness (Rev. 19:8).

But how could He know us so completely and still call us "lovely"? Here are five reasons:

You Are Lovely because of the Finished Work of Jesus on the Cross

Our loveliness comes from the wonderful gift of righteousness that is ours when we believe in Jesus (2 Cor. 5:21). We are lovely in Jesus's sight because of what He did for us in His death and resurrection, not what we do for Him. You are ready for the King's presence, because we have a King who gave away His beauty to take away our disfigurement. It is through the sacrifice of Christ that we are made lovely in God's sight. Our robe of righteousness that we wear has a designer label: "Made in Heaven Exclusively for the Bride of Christ."

Your Willing Spirit that Says Yes to God Makes You Lovely in His Eyes

The work of the Holy Spirit and our sincere intentions leave us lovely in God's sight. He will always define us not by our weak flesh but by the willing spirit. He knows our love is immature, but He sees more than the outward failures; He sees the beauty of His life forming within us. A contrite and willing spirit moves the heart of God. We can fail in many areas, but a broken heart He will not despise (Ps. 51:17).

The Kindness of God's Personality Shining through You Makes You Lovely

The passions and pleasures God feels toward us make us truly lovely in His eyes. He enjoys us even when we feel darkened by our failures and sins. The loveliness of His personality washes us in His presence and clothes us in the clean and glorious garments of salvation. You have absorbed His loveliness just by being near Him, communing with Him in His chamber.

Your Eternal Destiny of Becoming the Lamb's Wife Makes You Lovely

We are the ones loved by God because He has chosen us to be the spouse of His Son. The first time Jesus laid eyes upon you, He knew you would be His. What a mystery this truly is! Paul called it a "great mystery" concerning Christ becoming one with His bride (Eph. 5:31–32). God is not your Father-in-law; rather, He is your eternal Father-in-love. You are the love gift given to His Son (John 17:6).

You Possess Virtues of Grace that He Sees

You possess in the most secret and hidden places of your life beautiful virtues that will one day be seen by all. For now, they are only seeds of the glory and life of your Lord. But in time, they will spring up in radiant beauty. His image is stamped within you and is reflecting back to Him. Enriched with every grace and virtue, He sees beauty in your eyes and in the weaknesses of your life. Listen to the voice of your Father as you read this:

> Then I bathed you with water and washed off your blood from you and anointed you with oil. I clothed you also with embroidered cloth and shod you with fine leather. I wrapped you in fine linen and covered you with silk. And I adorned you with ornaments and put bracelets on your wrists and a chain on your neck. And I put a ring on your nose and earrings in your ears and a beautiful crown on your head. Thus you were adorned with gold and silver, and your clothing was of fine linen and silk and embroidered cloth. You ate fine flour and honey and oil. You grew exceedingly beautiful and advanced to royalty. And your renown went forth among the nations because of your beauty, for it was perfect through the splendor that I had bestowed on you, declares the Lord God (Ezekiel 16:9–14, NIV).

Pray this prayer today: "Father, You absolutely love me! The depths of Your love are beyond discovery. I am undone by Your love, overwhelmed by the immensity of Your passion to be with me and walk with me. Everything You do in my life makes me more beautiful in Your eyes. Thank You for Your fiery emotions of love for me and for all my family. Help me to absorb more of Your love today. Amen."

CHAPTER 4

GOD'S ILLOGICAL LOVE

**Please don't stare in scorn
because of my dark and sinful ways. (1:6)**

God's love is illogical. Paul states that it *"surpasses knowledge"* (Eph. 3:19). We can only know how God feels about us by revelation that comes from the Holy Spirit. The Holy Spirit must make it plain to our wounded souls: His love never fails. We are all fallen image-bearers, people who have marred the beauty of His image within us. We are destined for the throne yet made from dust, reaching for the sky yet bowing down in shame. All of us must discover that apart from Him our lives are earthbound and futile.

The day will come in your sacred journey that you feel like your "sin is showing." The Shulamite has begun to recognize this, as she exclaims, *"Please don't stare in scorn because of my dark and sinful ways."* Our natural inheritance in Adam left us with a darkened soul. How amazing it is that God takes this maiden and prepares her to be a glorious bride, transforming her by His tender love. It is time for an identity transplant to occur within her heart. Go ahead and ask Jesus how He sees *you.* I dare you.

The Shulamite is ashamed at the discovery of her defects.

She now realizes that others are aware of them too. She pleads, "Please, don't look at what's wrong with me. You might not like what You see." Self-conscious about her sin, and feeling like everyone is looking at her, she is miserable. What she truly wanted was to be presentable, to look good in the eyes of others.

Sound familiar? Have you ever felt like your "sin" is showing? When God exposes us as we are, it is proof that we are growing in our journey. But be careful not to let shame make you to be overly introspective and constantly analyzing how you seem to others. You were not meant to spend a lifetime with guilt as your companion. Jesus is to be your companion. You really are His beloved one, His favorite. There is a vast difference between knowing you are forgiven and knowing you are His favorite.

So who is the fairest of them all? Why, *you* are, in His sight. Jesus lives in you and will make your life into a radiant partner that will be at His side forever. Is this how you see yourself? Let Jesus speak right into your shame, your busyness, and your rejection. Hear Him tell you how fair you are to Him. Cherish His love.

We often look for mental answers, desiring to figure it all out, but God simply wants to touch our hearts with His fiery love. If we do figure it out, then we will always relate to God by our minds, not our hearts. Our King wants us to know Him in our heart, with the fullness of our passion. Love created us out of love, to share love with us.

But what about our relationships with others? Love will overcome their rejection and their misunderstanding of our sacred journey too:

My angry brothers quarreled with me
and appointed me guardian of their ministry vineyards,
yet I've not guarded my vineyard within. (1:6)

Who are the angry brothers sung about here? The crisis of rejection has come to the Shulamite through the angry words of others. Her youthful zeal to pursue Jesus wholeheartedly arouses the jealous anger of her brethren. There will be a time when our zeal for the Father's house will provoke others to jealousy (Ps. 69:8–9).

Often our zeal is without maturity, and we do silly things that cause others to reject us—yet even this is a test. The angry brothers take full advantage of her zeal and fervency. They overwork her in their fields. She becomes the keeper of *their* vineyards while her own vineyard is overgrown with weeds. She has not had time to make herself desirable for her Lover...she has been busy and overburdened with everyone's expectations. Has that been happening to you?

She kept other vineyards, but did not keep her own vineyard (heart). Our first responsibility before God is our own personal walk with Jesus, guarding and protecting and nourishing our own heart. Originally, what the Shulamite wanted most were the kisses of God's Word. However, as time went by, the weeds of spiritual coldness, sin, and shame choked her vineyard (garden of her heart). Taking care of her own vineyard means nurturing her personal communion with God and doing His will.

How easily we can be driven by a need for approval from others rather than our need for fellowship with Jesus. Anger, jealousy, and hard words are all a part of the old order of church life. God's true servants do not strive or speak harshly to those "keeping watch" over the flock.

Taking responsibilities apart from God's grace is a recipe for burnout. Overworked laborers in God's vineyard will be discouraged, and sometimes even quit. Weariness takes our joy and makes us feel guilty that we are not doing more for God. All of this becomes a religious yoke, which in time proves to be too heavy on our shoulders. However, Jesus is easy to please. He is coupled to us—united to us in the yoke of love. A yoke of religious responsibilities is simply too heavy to bear. As we are newly awakened to fervency, however, we become vulnerable to the false yokes of the church. When we find our identity in what *we do* for God, instead of *intimacy with Christ*, we can lose our vision.

The vineyard of others drained the Shulamite's spiritual life, leaving her own inner life in God neglected. Your life in the Spirit is a vineyard, a garden for the Lord. To neglect your own vineyard is to abandon your call to pursue Jesus with an undistracted love. Cultivating the heart is a daily responsibility that must be taken seriously.

It is the strategy of the Devil to sidetrack you from your pure devotion to God. If he can keep you exhausted and overloaded with a religious yoke, he knows that in time your life of intimacy with Jesus will suffer. It is easy to blame the angry brothers, but truly we are the ones who have grown cold.

Others will try to tell you that you can't afford to take the time to be alone with God. Like Martha before you, they will expect you to cook dinner and get the house ready for Him to show up. They may even misunderstand that you are being drawn into a life of passionate pursuit of God; yet all of this only refines our motives. The day will come when our own vineyard (inner life) will be refreshing and our labors for God will not be to impress people, but will be from the overflow of His life in us. He will become our very great reward.

> **Won't you tell me, Lover of my soul,**
> **where do you feed your flock?**
> **Where do you lead your beloved ones**
> **to rest in the heat of the day? (1:7)**

"Won't you tell me, Lover of my soul..." The Shulamite realizes now that it is not the church or others she primarily loves; it is Him whom she loves. Loneliness is leaving her soul as their paths merge. She must have Him and Him alone. Her thoughts turn away from her to the one she loves. If only she knew where she could find Him:

> **Tell me...**
> **where do you feed your flock?**

Where do you lead your beloved ones
to rest in the heat of the day? (1:7)

In the darkness of her experience, she wants to know where He leads His flock at noon when the sun is the brightest. Midday is a season of light and glory. The Shulamite longs to be in the midday brightness with her Shepherd. She is saying, "I have been fed by others, but I am still empty. My hunger is for You, not just teachings *about* You. Bring me into Your midday light of revelation, untroubled by darkness. Take me there. I am weary with *doing stuff* (keeping vineyards), but now I want to rest in Your shadow. Where do you rest Your sheep? Take me *there*."

The exquisite love of Jesus is a fountain that will never dry up. You can drink your fill, and you can drink it repeatedly. This is where Jesus rests His flock at midday, at His fountain of delight. Now she sees this King as a Shepherd—a gentle, satisfying Shepherd.

Shepherd. What a fitting name for Jesus: *"The Lord is my best friend and my shepherd"* (Ps. 23:1). He will lead His flock into the perfect pasture, the green pasture where we will grow the most. The pasture for you is measured according to the hunger that you possess. The poetry of the heart is spoken as the Shulamite opens her life to be fed as one of His flock, resting under the midday glory. She is ready to feed her own soul with Him (Matt. 11:28–29).

For I wish to be wrapped all around you,
as I go among the flocks of your under-shepherds.
It is you I long for, with no veil between us! (1:7)

She acknowledges, "Why should I seek others when I must have You?" The Hebrew text describes her as "a wandering woman." She asks the Shepherd why she should continue to be like a veiled woman wandering in shame. Her cry is for the Bridegroom to take away her shame (Isa. 4:1). You and I must have an unveiled face before the Lord. Shame is a veil that will keep us from seeing Him clearly. When we are ashamed, our gaze is on our self, our failures, our weaknesses. It is time to lift the veil and gaze on Him undistracted. Only the Shepherd can remove the veil of shame from the human heart, not just His friends (His ministers). The maiden's willingness to serve has been used by others.

Jesus longs that we would pray this prayer. He does not want us to give up and give in to a spiritually dull life in God. He does not want us to write ourselves off as hopeless hypocrites. So pray this prayer today: "Feed my heart like You used to. I feel like there is a veil between us at times. It makes me feel like I love You from a distance. My own vineyard has weeds in it. Many things are going wrong. Come and help me this day. Come close to me today. I need to touch You, the one whom I love."

But what do you do when Jesus feels distant? The Shepherd-King says to the Shulamite:

> **Listen, my radiant one—**
> **if you ever lose sight of me**
> **just follow in my footsteps where I lead my lovers.**
> **Come with your burdens and cares.**
> **Come to the place near the sanctuary of my shepherds—**
> **there you will find me. (1:8)**

The tender Shepherd is compassionate in her weakness (James 5:11). Others would have rebuked her for being too busy, too distracted. But the words He continually speaks in this soliloquy of the soul, the Song of Songs, is to call the immature maiden His *"radiant one."* There is none more kind and gentle than He.

True prophetic ministry is the voice of Jesus speaking to His bride the testimony He wants to speak over us (Rev. 19:10). He is infinitely kind to those who fail. The bruises of life are healed by His kind touch. That the King would call this goat-smelling, sun-darkened maiden the loveliest of women is simply unbelievable. He describes His bride-to-be as "radiant" although she could only see herself darkened by sin, feeling distant from Him.

If you ever lose sight of me... (1:8)

His answer shocks many people who read these words, even today. We would expect a rebuke to be given here. He knows our garden isn't being kept and that we serve Him at a distance; however, we are still radiant to Him. He calls us radiant even in the midst of our disorientation and failure. We might be unlovely to the angry sons, but we are beautiful and radiant to Him. We may despise ourselves, but we are radiant to Him. He speaks this directly into her shame and rejection.

The Shulamite's cry for the Shepherd made her radiant in His sight. Jesus does not just see the sinful struggle that we have in our lives; He sees the seeking heart. He does not define us by the unkempt vineyard we display, but by the budding virtues yet to grow into fullness. How kind is our Shepherd! We are safe with a friend like this one.

We must see ourselves as in a process of becoming a look-alike partner of the Son of God. Today, Christ truly sees me as fully perfected. He does not see my hypocrisy and He does not see my double-mindedness. He has intentionally limited His own vision, so as to place my sins as far from His sight as the east is from the west. I am washed clean and perfected. Dwelling in the consciousness of His adoration over my beauty is the thing that continually draws my heart into His life.

It is so important we know that we are lovely in His sight. The power of hope is released when we drink of these words. Knowing we are loved while unworthy builds a fortress around our own souls. Doubt, fear, and accusation cannot take root in us. When we are tempted to quit out of self-disgust and condemnation, it is this revelation that redeems us: "Listen, My radiant one, because you seek Me even in your weakness." The great secret of your heart that God will someday reveal is not your sin, but your fervent love for Him that would not give up in your search for Him (1 Cor. 4:5).

Pray this prayer today: "Lord God, You know everything there is to know about me. Yet You still love me with endless love. I want my heart to soak in Your words today, 'Listen, My radiant one.' Continue Your work in my heart until radiance shines through my doubts and my discouragement. I take Your words as my life and my strength. In Jesus's name I pray, amen."

CHAPTER 5

THE RADIANT ONE

**Listen, my radiant one—
if you ever lose sight of me
just follow in my footsteps where I lead my lovers.
Come with your burdens and cares.
Come to the place near the sanctuary of my shepherds—
there you will find me. (1:8)**

The Shepherd-King gives the Shulamite an unexpected answer to help her know where she could find Him. He instructs her to *"follow in my footsteps where I lead my lovers."* He is saying to her, "You will not find Me in the busy streets of the world." Rather, we are to just follow His lovers who hear His voice (John 10:27–28).

At times we lose our way, thus needing examples to follow. We need direction. We need an answer. What will He tell us? It is time to get involved with the body of Christ, with others who are on their own sacred journey. The Shulamite cannot draw back from body life just because the angry brothers wounded her. If she is to find the Shepherd's resting place, she must reconnect to the flock He leads. The Devil wants us in isolation, separating us from others who know and hear God's voice. If the enemy cannot overwork us with premature responsibilities, he will keep us isolated and wounded.

The wise Shepherd encourages the Shulamite to reconnect with a flock that follows Him. Others are in pursuit of Him—get in step with them and move on. Simply stated: Jesus wants you to stay committed to the body of Christ. The woundings of your heart are your tests to mature your faith. If you have been hurt on the killing fields of the church, you must move on with His flock, regardless of how you were treated in the past. When the angry brothers mistreat us, our temptation is to leave the church and isolate ourselves. "Lord, I only want You," is our cry. "I will never let anyone hurt me again."

Sadly, many in the church today have made inner vows never to be open again to others, especially spiritual leaders. These inner vows must someday be broken, making us vulnerable again. We find the Shepherd with His sheep, His *corporate* bride, not just individuals. So often we will only find the Shepherd when we are in sweet fellowship with His people.

"Come with your burdens and cares." The Shulamite bride must come and bring her burdens and cares to Him and stay connected to those who love Him. And He also invites her, *"Come to the place near the sanctuary of my shepherds—there you will find me."* There is an ancient proverb that says, "If you wish to smell pleasant, stand near those who sell perfume." You will find the Lord near the "tents" of godly leaders.

Those who are in pursuit of Jesus must have an open spirit to their leaders. As we discover the grace to relate to imperfect shepherds, we discover Him in deeper and ever-expanding ways. God is the one who chooses His shepherds. They are the ones who will lead us to Him. It is important that we draw life from others who follow our King. If we have a know-it-all attitude and remain unteachable, then we will miss the one we are looking for.

So far the Shulamite has had to experience:

- The sense of shame over her "dark" ways and human failures.

- The rejection of "angry brothers."
- Being overworked with religious duties and expectations.
- Distraction has caused her garden-heart to be full of weeds.
- Jesus seems to be distant. Her service is without intimacy.

But the Lord of love knows just what fuel we need in our tank to see us through the difficult times of disorientation and failure. He knows all the pressure she is enduring and still He calls her beautiful and radiant. How He loves His bride. The preparation we need is found in His caresses. He says to her:

My dearest one… (1:9)

Jesus comes to her as the most kind Shepherd. This is how we also find Him when we ask Him into our lives—so gentle, pleasing, and compassionate. He is all that and more—much more. In this season of life, the maiden is pleased with how He satisfies her, how deeply His words touch her heart. But she hasn't a clue as to what lies ahead…only that He is with her, and she is happy to have Him at her side.

Once again the Bridegroom sings this sublime song of love to her heart. With supreme tenderness He speaks to her every time with words like, *"My dearest one," "lovely,"* or *"radiant one."* This shows the heart of God toward us even while we are immature. Weak people touch the heart of God. His affection toward us is beyond our understanding, beyond our performance, and is rooted in what He has done for us, not what we can do for Him.

The word *dearest one* is literally lover-friend or darling. You have the beautiful privilege of becoming the lover-friend of the Son of God. Every time He looks at you, He is thrilled with your seeking heart. Let no one take this truth from you. Think about it for a moment: Jesus calls us "dearest one." He is tender beyond words, kind to us when we still feel ugly and sinful. No one on earth speaks this way to us when we fail. These divine kisses are what will sustain her in the wilderness, just like they sustain us in our wilderness wanderings.

Luke wrote two books in the New Testament, the gospel of Luke and the book of Acts. They were addressed to one named Theophilus, which means "lover of God." Beloved, it is doubtful there was a man named Theophilus who received Luke and Acts as a letter. They were written to you, "most excellent lover of God" (Luke 1:1–4; Acts 1:1).

This means you must begin to place your name over the writings of the Bible and realize that it was all written as a love letter to you, the fiancée of Jesus Christ. Too many of us are working frantically to earn the right to stay in His kingdom. We need to rest in knowing that we are His darling, His favorite one.

Jesus is determined to leap over the mountains of fear and jump over our walls of insecurity until He has fully captured our hearts in love. When this grips us, we will no longer strive to make God like us, winning His approval with good behavior.

Knowing how God sees you is the true healing balm of the wounded heart. Everything else, every program and therapy, is only a Band-Aid. God's love heals. It casts out fear and brings in confidence. His deep affection removes loneliness and rejection from our heart. His overwhelming love overcomes our insecurities and makes us whole again.

The Shepherd-King says:

> **Let me tell you how I see you—**
> **you are so thrilling to me.**
> **To gaze upon you is like looking**
> **at one of Pharaoh's finest horses—**
> **a strong, regal steed pulling his royal chariot. (1:9)**

The Bridegroom calls His bride a horse. Is this a compliment? How would you like to be called a horse? What does He mean by this? Could it be that her strong desire to follow Him is like the strength of the finest horse pulling a king's chariot? In ancient poetry, the horse was always used as an emblem of beauty and inner strength. Her strong passion to know Him is like the strength of a racehorse pulling Pharaoh's chariot.

Historians write of the chariot of Pharaoh, telling us it was embossed with pure gold, so that when the sun shone upon it, its glare would blind the armies of the enemy. The royal, golden chariot was only drawn by the most beautiful of horses. Jesus is saying to you here: "Let Me tell you what I think of you. Your brave desire to follow Me is beautiful in My sight. Your elegant strength to do righteousness is much more intense than you realize. I see your hidden potential. You may feel like a failure, but I see you as the strong mare harnessed to My heart."

Beloved, you thrill His heart. You have been trained like Pharaoh's horses to carry the King Himself. You are not offensive to Him; you are beautiful to Him! You are as swift and as strong as a racehorse to run after Him. You see, Jesus holds a crown over your head and lets you grow up into it.

The Shulamites are the horses of fire that pull the Ark—they are overcomers in God's sight (Zech. 10:3). Like a horse in the day of battle are His people. Joel's army has the appearance of horses in the day of battle (Joel 2:4). Have you ever thought that the victorious church is the white horse that will bring back the King: *"Look! He advances like the clouds, his chariots come like a whirlwind, and his horses are swifter than eagles"* (Jer. 4:13, NIV). Your destiny is to be the mighty horse of fire that laughs at fear and is afraid of nothing, that cannot stand still when the trumpet sounds; you will catch the scent of battle from afar and will leap at the battle cry (Job 39:19–25).

Pray this prayer today: "Thank You, Father, that You are making me strong in Your grace. Your love surrounds me this day and makes me confident and secure. I want to always be fastened to Your heart and to reflect Your glory through my life. I yield my heart to You, today and always. In Jesus's name, amen."

CHAPTER 6

WE WILL ENHANCE YOUR BEAUTY

Your tender cheeks are aglow—
your earrings and gem-laden necklaces set them ablaze.
We will enhance your beauty,
encircling you with our golden reins of love.
You will be marked with our redeeming grace. (1:10–11)

The Lord designed you to be emotional. Jesus made every human being to have emotions that only He could fill and direct toward His heart. A denial of our emotions is a denial of who we were made to be in Christ Jesus. Jesus touches our emotions by His Spirit—this is how He made us; this is how we were made to work. This King has touched the Shulamite's emotional makeup. He sees her fervency toward Him and calls it beautiful. You may think others are strange when they show their emotions toward Jesus, but He calls it beautiful. She cries out, *"Draw me,"* (1:4) and He draws her heart toward Himself.

"Your tender cheeks are aglow." The cheeks, or countenance, speak of our emotions. Emotions are revealed by our countenance. Anger, joy, sadness, and shame are always seen on the cheeks, for this is where we express what is inside of us. When He calls her cheeks beautiful, He acknowledges her tender emotions toward

Him. She has a beautiful smile. He is delighted with her! Did you know that your emotions are attractive to God? Your Creator loves the smile He puts on you.

"Your tender cheeks are aglow—your earrings…set them ablaze." Jesus is the artist, the craftsman of every heart. He adorns us in His grace to be beautiful in His sight (Isa. 61:3). These earrings are the grace gifts that He has placed upon us that we might have beauty before Him. We are gorgeous to Him! *"The King is enthralled by your beauty"* (Ps. 45:11). He loves to make His bride beautiful by giving her ears to hear His voice and a heart to respond to what He is speaking.

"Your…gem-laden necklaces set them ablaze." The necklaces adorn the neck, which speaks of the will. We can be "stiff-necked" (a sign of a stubborn will), or we can bow the neck, which is a sign of submission and reverence. The neck is what turns the head and directs the body, while our will is what chooses the path we walk along. The jewels on her neck speak of royalty and authority. She has said yes to God and is resolute to follow this King. When Jesus looks upon you, He sees the yes in your spirit, even though you may have seasons of failure. He sees your will submitted to learn the lessons of growing in God. Every time you say yes to Him, another jewel, or pearl, is added to your authority. He sees you as one who has acquired a gentleness to submit to Him, making you lovely in His sight.

"Necklaces" can also be translated as "chains of gold." Golden chains upon our neck—we are love slaves to Jesus our King! The chains of gold speak of royal authority, for only a king had chains of gold. In those days, few people could afford a chain of gold besides a king, which meant they were rare and expensive. A prince would wear a chain of gold with the king's emblem on it as he walked through the town.

The Trinity is involved in maturing a bride for Jesus. Father, Son, and Holy Spirit are the ones who will shape your identity, not your friends or your past. Listen to the voice of the Godhead speaking to you: *"We will enhance your beauty, encircling you with our golden reins of love."* The beautiful Godhead is committed to making *you* beautiful.

Gold in the Scriptures points to the divine character. The day will come when the maiden will be Christlike, made in the image of His character. This is the grace-work of God. He makes us like gold as we continue in our sacred journey in the grace of God. The heart of an extravagant worshiper of Jesus is like refined gold. He promises her that where she lacks, He will supply. The Bridegroom promises to complete the work of refining her heart. It is Jesus's responsibility to make you shine like gold. God promises to work on you if you will not give up. You are only a failure in life if you quit. You will be one who moves on until His gold is found in you.

As the king surrounded me,
the sweet fragrance of my praise perfume awakened the night.
(1:12)

Her perfume (spikenard) begins to spread its fragrance as her spontaneous worship begins to fill the room, and the revelation of the cross expands her heart. This is a King beyond belief. His abundance releases praise as adoration ascends from her heart to God.* Her thoughts are, "How can I honor and treat Him in a way worthy of His love?" Forgetting about herself, her praise-perfume ascends into the atmosphere.

Feeding on the truths of the cross will always release worship from our hearts. To receive and enjoy all that God provides for us is the path to adoration. We have an exotic perfume to share with our King. We can bring enjoyment to the heart of Jesus as He receives our praise. Jesus enjoys the aroma of adoration as we gaze on Him in worship. Our praise-perfume ascends to God like

---

* It was while Jesus and His friends were "reclining at the table" that Mary of Bethany, the extravagant lover, poured out her expensive spikenard perfume upon His feet.

incense before the altar of heaven (Rev. 5:8). On the wings of love our honor and worship surround Him and satisfy Him.

The Corinthian church was the most carnal (fleshly) in the New Testament. It was to them that Paul wrote: *"For we are to God the pleasing aroma of Christ"* (2 Cor. 2:15, NIV). Immature saints who worship out of their brokenness release the sweetest perfume into heaven—the fragrance of Christ. The virtues of Jesus come forth as we worship God from a tender and pure heart.

What kind of fragrance is coming from your spirit before God? Does God smell the fragrance of confidence and gratitude? Many can say, "I am dark in my heart," but they lack the understanding to also say, "I am lovely to God." Our perfumed worship arises through the day, as we say, "I love You."

In Luke 7, the prostitute poured out spikenard upon the feet of the Lord Jesus. This was her act of worshiping the Son of God out of her brokenness. The spiritual perfume she released thrilled the heart of Jesus as He witnessed her devotion that was shown through kisses and tears. She was unguarded in her devotion of love to the King.

So many times we guard our heart, we hide our emotions, trying our best to keep them private. But God longs for us to unveil our heart and be extravagant in our worship of Him. We cast aside condemnation and pride, throwing ourselves into His arms with love exchanged deeply between our hearts—His love and our love mingled into one fragrance.

Those who have been forgiven much, worship much. Have you been forgiven much? Can you worship Him right where you are today, even in a place of brokenness? Pour out your love to Him and you'll have more love to receive from Him.

Pray this prayer today: "Jesus, like Mary of Bethany, I pour out my praises like perfume upon Your feet. Your love for me is more than I can comprehend. Receive my love for You. Draw it up into Your heart. Let it rise before You as sacred incense. I love You more than words can tell. Amen."

CHAPTER 7

LIKE A BUNDLE
OF MYRRH

**A sachet of myrrh is my lover,
like a tied-up bundle of myrrh resting over my heart. (1:13)**

The Shulamite begins to smell something as she pours out her praises to Jesus. It smells sweet, but what is it exactly? Is it her spikenard? No, it's myrrh that she smells. Her perfume has been completely overwhelmed by the fragrance of myrrh. She smells the sufferings of Christ.

Myrrh is an expensive perfume used by the wealthy as a burial spice. Jacob sent myrrh down to Egypt as one of the choice and costly products of the land. The wise kings who visited Jesus presented gold, frankincense, and myrrh as a prophetic sign of Christ's majesty—embalming spice was given to Jesus at His birth. Myrrh is also a symbol of His death, His cross that He would ultimately die on. It was mixed with wine and offered to Jesus while He hung on the cross. When Mary came to the tomb of Jesus, she brought with her myrrh. Jesus was born with myrrh and buried with myrrh. And it is mentioned eight times in the Song of Songs.

But there is no amount of myrrh that could be compared to the costly sacrifice of Jesus on the cross. All of His garments smelled of myrrh (Ps. 45:8). The Hebrew word for *myrrh* is a form of the word *bitter*. The ancient Hebrew teachers describe myrrh as "tears from a tree." It is from the sacred tree that liquid love pours down, whispering, "It is finished."

Myrrh speaks of the reality of embracing the cross and the end of our fleshly ways. Some wealthy women in the ancient world went to bed with a bundle or large necklace of myrrh to provide fragrance throughout the night. Solomon gave the Shulamite this extravagantly expensive gift. The bride proclaimed that Jesus was like a bundle of myrrh that laid on her heart through the night. The cross was King Jesus's extravagantly expensive gift to His bride. Jesus's death was an "abundant offering," speaking what He endured because of His love for us. It reveals how valuable we are to Him. Our value is seen in what Jesus endured for us.

The cross is a bundle of myrrh. As the maiden first catches the scent of myrrh, she begins to understand what following the King will cost her. What if following Him brings pain and sacrifice? What if it will mean rejection and misunderstanding and dying to our own strength? But every Shulamite cries out, "He is worth it! My Lover is to me a sachet of myrrh resting between my breasts." The maiden reveals her bridal spirit by her willingness to follow Jesus at all costs. The dimensions of His leadership have penetrated her inwardly. She will embrace Him as a bundle of myrrh.

A bundle is something that is tied up and bound. Jesus was tied up and nailed to the cross as a bundle of myrrh for you and for me. A bundle of lovely virtues is our Lord Jesus! He is a marvelous variety of Prophet, Priest, King, Husband, Shepherd, and Friend. We take the bundle of His virtue into our hearts—His gentleness, courage, compassion, strength, and unfailing kindness. His suffering love is like the fragrance of myrrh.

The cross will make us beautiful and sweet smelling. As we draw near to the place of sacrifice and adore the one who gave it all away to save the world, the fragrant scent of myrrh is upon us. Others will recognize that we have been with Him.

He is like a bouquet of henna blossoms—
henna plucked near the vines at the fountain of the Lamb.
I will hold him and never let him part. (1:14)

Jesus is the loveliest flower filled with sweet fragrance. His beauty captivates our souls. The maiden discovers, after meditation on the cross, how lovely this King truly is. Even His sufferings become sweetness and delightful to every tender heart. When we see by inward revelation how beautiful He truly is, we can never go on the way we were before—we become lovers of God, longing for His beauty.

The Hebrew word for *henna* is *kopher*, which can also be translated as atonement. Jewish teachers in ancient times believed the phrase "a cluster of henna blossoms" is a reference to the Messiah. They translated it as "a man who atones for all." The fragrance of Christ's atonement for all our sins is a sweet fragrance indeed. Why doesn't the world see His beauty? He is not a burdensome, heavy-handed King. He is not the religious god of the Pharisees. Rather, He is the Prince of life, the splendor and glory of God. With fresh revelation we must convey to others that He is our dream come true.

There is one who is so altogether lovely, so incredibly faithful and true, that your heart is safe in His care. He is not just a flower, but a *"bouquet"* of flowers! His beauty comes from every aspect of His character. You could never take it all in, even if you lived for all eternity. He is a cluster of beauty before your heart. Have you ever found another who is so tender with your weaknesses? He understands your failures completely, yet passionately embraces you anyway.

"At the fountain of the Lamb." Jesus is pleasant, like the smell of henna in the midst of a vineyard. The Hebrew is actually "Engedi," which means "fountain of the Lamb." Engedi was an oasis alongside the Dead Sea, its vineyards yielded some of the greatest fragrances in the land of Israel. These blossoms of

henna from Engedi speak of the most intense fragrance imaginable—the tenderness and beauty of Jesus intoxicates the soul.*

The Shulamite's one theme now is that this wonderful King loves her as she is. The day will come in *your* life when you will know that He has total ownership of your heart as well. You exist for Him alone, without consideration of your comforts or your pleasures. With a focus entirely on Him, you will see yourself as His desired one, His beloved. What a love-theology this truly is! Soon every Shulamite will understand more fully what that means.

Pray this prayer today as you take communion: "Lord Jesus, I love the cross on which You died. Your sacrifice is like the fragrance of myrrh. The way that You loved me more than Your own blood stirs my soul. I take You into my life again. Your pierced body and the blood-wounds of the cross draw me closer to the mystery of Your love. Help me express today this love by the way I live and by the way I speak. Amen."

---

* *Henna* is a Hebrew homonym that can also mean "atonement" or "redeeming grace."

CHAPTER 8

HIS DIVINE AFFECTION

Look at you, my dearest darling,
you are so lovely!
You are beauty itself to me.
Your passionate eyes are like loyal, gentle doves. (1:15)

Words like these wash over our souls. And when we understand who is saying it, our minds cannot comprehend it. Jesus, the radiant Son, calls you lovely. He calls you His darling, His fair one, His true friend. He affirms the maiden in her worship, in her new revelation of the cross. He responds to her and to you with the affirmation of divine affection: *"You are so lovely!"*

Jesus doesn't just say, "You are lovely." He says, "You are *so* lovely!" Most of us, if we are honest with ourselves, do not see ourselves as lovely. What does Jesus see in us then, that He would call us lovely? In particular, why would He call *me* lovely? A radical love like this cannot be explained; it can only be enjoyed. Who can explain the power of a lover's kiss? There are things in God not meant to be understood; they are to be received by faith and cherished. He has given us all things (including the revelation of His love) to be enjoyed (1 Tim. 6:17). We see this revelation poetically portrayed in the Song of Songs. Beloved, it will take forever for the mind to catch up with what God has put in our spirits.

Believers sometimes say that the church is ugly, messed up, and full of problems. Others could look at you and me and say the same thing. Many Christians look at how God loves and blesses those they struggle with, and so they pray: "Lord, don't You see how much so-and-so has hurt me? Don't You see how bad, how immature, how messed up they are?" But Jesus looks beyond the momentary mess to see into the motives of the heart. The longing of the bride is for Him. This is what thrills His heart and causes Him to tell her again how lovely she is. God can look at the very people you see as ugly and call them lovely. Where you see blemishes, He sees beauty.

All our lives we seek the love of others and feel that we need them to survive, when it is only *His* love that brings true satisfaction and healing. But the healing love of Jesus comes when we understand that we are born again in Christ Jesus, who calls us beautiful even while we are immature. We are convinced He sees our sins and failures, but actually what fills His heart are thoughts of desire and mercy. God's thoughts of love for you outnumber the grains of sand on all the seashores on this planet. And all these thoughts, the deep thoughts of God, are for your blessing, your benefit, and are filled with love. He chose you before the foundation of the world to be His. That means that God has had a long time to think about you. He has had the experience of knowing you and loving you before you were even born!* For billions and billions of years, God has been thinking about loving you. The Holy Spirit searches out those archives of the thoughts of God's love for you and makes them real at precisely the right time—if you are listening.

We know that we will radiate beauty in heaven for all eternity,

---

* See Psalm 139:17–18; Jeremiah 29:11; 1 Corinthians 2:9–11; Ephesians 1:4.

yet we struggle to recognize the beauty Jesus sees in us today. The Devil will call us a hopeless hypocrite. The enemy wears down many with accusations and condemnation. He wants us to feel hopeless so we will give up. How many times do we spend excessive emotional energy fighting the fires of condemnation and worthlessness? Through our shame and preoccupation with failure, we hear the words: *"You are beauty itself to me!"* Can you see the Lord looking down on you full of admiration, saying: "O, I love you. I find delight in you—you fill Me with such pleasure! Listen to Me, child—I call you lovely!"

My beloved one,
you are pleasing beyond words,
and so winsome! (1:16)

The more we see of Jesus's beauty and the more we love Him, the more spiritual pleasure we experience in our walk with God. The more He speaks words of love to our weak hearts, the more glorious He becomes in our eyes. Love releases revelation to our hearts. With an unguarded spirit, our hearts open up to the words of the King. We begin to take notice of this loving King. As the Shulamite is washed by love, what will our response be to this revelation? The Shulamite adores Jesus more than ever before! Don't you?

The key to growing in God is receiving the revelation of His love (Eph. 3:18). The fourfold dimension of this love brings the fullness of Jesus into our lives. We will never grow in God apart from a context of being enjoyed by Him. Worship must flow from a heart captured by this love. The loveliness of the King penetrates the Shulamite's spirit. Jesus is becoming more and more attractive to her. He is not the harsh, driving master that she imagined Him to be. Religious lies told her to keep her guard up, to cringe when she came near Him. But now she discovers His glorious tenderness, even in her immaturity and weakness.

Jesus satisfies. No one is as kind as He. To believe He is not kind is nothing but a lie that keeps other people away from Him. There is never unkindness or harshness with Him. His commands are not burdensome; they are life-giving. Every feature about this Prince is glorious. The bride-to-be is making a new discovery of how trustworthy He is to her, and there is an exchange of deep affection between the two of them at this moment. As they lock eyes with each other, a love that lasts a lifetime is birthed.

When you see Jesus's lovely face, it is so right to fall in love with Him. It is so right to go anywhere He sends you. It is so right to give up all other pursuits to follow Him and Him alone. When we expect and deserve a lecture, He stoops to kiss us. When we fully expect the clenched fist, He opens His palm to show us the nail scars He has in His hands. What a charming King He is! Who would not love Him?

Jesus will one day present to Himself a *"radiant church"* (Eph. 5:27). With the revelation of a cherishing love, the stains of our past will be removed. There will be no shame or blemish upon us as love will wash and glorify us, perfecting us in holiness. The secret of becoming radiant is the secret of His holy love. The more we receive this nourishing and cherishing love, the more "radiance" will come upon us on our journey into His heart. We truly become radiant with the life of Christ shining through the joy of being loved. Radiance is in our future.

The Greek word used in Ephesians 5:27 for this "radiant church" is *endoxos*. This can also be translated as "gorgeous, honorable, esteemed, splendid, and infused with glory!" This is what love will do to you, rearranging your future from gloom to glory. Nothing can transform you more completely than this cherishing love of a Bridegroom who defines you not by your attainments but by your adorable beauty.

**Our resting place is anointed and flourishing,
like a green forest meadow bathed in light.
Rafters of cedar branches are over our heads**

and balconies of pleasant-smelling pines.
A perfect home! (1:16–17)

You have been seated with Christ in heavenly places—there is no better resting place than this (Eph. 2:6). The maiden has the revelation of the luxurious resting-place given to her by the King. He has made her lie down in green (verdant) forest meadows like the pastures found in Psalm 23, forever resting in His anointing and love. Flourishing in His grace and bathed in the light of His revelation! The New American Standard Bible translates this, *"our luxuriant couch."*

The Shulamite has found a resting place in the presence of God, all because of the abundance of His love. She speaks of "our *resting place*," for she sees the truth of being a coheir with Him. The cross has now become her resting place. In the sanctuary of His sweet heart, we rest and abide. What a soft, safe bed is the Bridegroom's heart. The King has shown her the green room in His palace, the place of growth, maturity, and rest. This room shall be ours forever. As the Shulamite looks around the room, she glances up and says, *"Rafters of cedar branches are over our heads."*

Cedar is a hard wood. As she journeys toward life union with this King, strength and safety are all around the Shulamite maiden. She sees the security of *"our house"* and rests safely with Him. This is the eternal and glorious house of intimacy. The cedar tree is an emblem of life and the cypress or fir is a symbol of death, for they were used to make caskets. Both the cedar and the fir were the two major building materials in Solomon's temple. They speak of the life and death of our Lord Jesus that has become our security and covering.

Rafters of cedar branches are over our heads
and balconies of pleasant-smelling pines. (1:17)

The word *rafters* literally means "galleries" or "balconies." These are the porches that extend out from the house, the enclosed deck.

The bride and Bridegroom sit and walk together in sweet fellowship on a balcony made of cedar, a fragrant and durable wood. We have found a perfect home within the heart of our Bridegroom as we rest in Him in this place.

The house is the church, the house of the Lord (1 Tim. 3:15). The bride is now ready to enter back into fellowship with others. She understands that He is her resting place and security. Her heart has been overwhelmed with His expressions of love, but now she must face new tests and grow in her journey toward Christlikeness. But first she must embrace her true identity.

Jesus has given us His beauty and His house. The bride's response to the revelation of being loved and beautiful to God (1:15) is to see with dove's eyes. The maiden sees Jesus as handsome (the beautiful God), as the one she loves (Beloved), and pleasant as He leads her life to rest and security now and eternal glory in the age to come. Abiding in Jesus's love brings her abundant rest and confidence in her life (1:16). Have you found that abiding place, fresh and flourishing in His presence?

God is building an enduring house for His bride, the church. And His dwelling place is strong, permanent, and durable. This is the reason Jesus became a Man, so that He could provide a permanent dwelling place fit for His beautiful bride. And she sees the house as "our house," or their dwelling place together forever (Eph. 2:19–22; 1 Peter 2:5). It's strong, beautiful, and forever. To the end of our days, we will forever dwell in His beauty and strength.

Pray this prayer today: "Jesus, I want to be a part of Your radiant bride. Change me from the inside out so that my life matches the words of love You have spoken over me. I thank You that all my sins have been washed away by Your loving grace. Help me to find my resting place in You, no matter what happens this day. I want the peace of knowing that I am hidden in You, sheltered in Your love, strengthened by Your might. Thank You for being the perfect one, the only one for me. Amen."

CHAPTER 9

THE ROSE OF SHARON

**I am truly his rose,
the very theme of his song. (2:1)**

Handpicked, that's who you are. Handpicked by Jesus to be His perfect partner forever and a day. This is your chosen destiny, to be so close and so radiant that you become a full-time advertisement for His glory. The Father has given a rose to His Son. The truth is that there is only one rose that Jesus longs for, an intoxicating and beautiful one, full of His glory. This is the fullness of everything Jesus desires outside of the Trinity—it is the bride of Christ. The church must begin to see herself as His rose. The riches of redemption have been freely given, the robe of righteousness is upon us—we are the rose of Sharon.

Scholars are split over who is speaking here—is it the King or the maiden? Although many of us have adored Jesus as the Rose of Sharon, it is clearly the maiden here who confesses her new identity in Jesus—she calls herself *"a rose of Sharon."* Beloved, you are His rosebud. As she calls herself *His rose,* the maiden is beginning to see that she is His inheritance; the one who brings pleasure and enjoyment to His heart. She is the inheritance the

Father promised to give to His Son. You too are God's love gift to Jesus.

It's time for you to see yourself as a rose of Sharon, the great prize promised to Jesus. Some scholars have taught that the name *Sharon* could be translated "His song." The maiden suddenly realizes that she is the theme (rose) of His song. The singing King has plucked His rosebud and held her to His heart. It is time to no longer see yourself as unworthy of His love, but as a rose that intoxicates the heart of our Lord. You are the theme of His song, His rose of Sharon.

The Father cultivated this rose for His Son. With tender care, the God of heaven caused the rose to grow and open its blossom to the love of the Son. This rose represents the fullness of everything Jesus desires—you have fully won His heart! The bondage of false humility will always disqualify you. It is unbelief to say, "I am not worthy" when Jesus says, "You are without flaw, My love." The lies of accusation were silenced by the banging, clanging sound of the nails piercing the perfect one who takes away our flaws. There is nothing left to do but say yes when He calls you worthy. There is nothing left to do but say yes when He tells you to go and represent Him fully in His love and power. It is not presumption to accept the place that grace has given us in His eyes.

When you were blind to your sins and had no vision of the beauty of Christ, you could say you were unworthy, much like the prodigal son who left everything and wasted it upon himself in the far country. But when the Father's arms are around you and the Father's kisses are on your cheek and His robe of glory is upon you as the feast of love begins, it would be wrong to say, "I am unworthy." All has changed; you are feasting at His table and covered with His grace.

When you understand that you are His rose, difficulties don't matter any longer, for there is an anchor of hope that holds you. When you are overwhelmed in your weakness, you are still His rosebud. The rose of Christ is now your identity. The end-time church will soon confess that we are His rose. Like a rose that has blossomed in the wilderness, the bride will see herself as the cherished of His heart (Isa. 35:1–2).

The Shulamite says:

> **I'm overshadowed by his love,**
> **growing in the valley! (2:1)**

Then the Shepherd-King responds:

> **Yes, you are my darling companion.**
> **You stand out from all the rest.**
> **For though the curse of sin surrounds you,**
> **still you remain as pure as a lily,**
> **even more than all others. (2:2)**

You are like a lily *"growing in the valley."* In the deepest valleys of our lives, we are still united to Jesus Christ, *"overshadowed by his love."* Our love for Him cannot be taken from us in the valley, for He sees us as His rose and His lily. Lilies speak of purity. As Jesus's lovely lily, the maiden-bride acknowledges that she is pure in His sight. *You* are the one lily who sparkles with dew in the eyes of Jesus the Bridegroom. This is true even in the low and dark places of your life, as well as when things seem to be going fine. Your whole life can be redefined when you claim this as your identity: *"For though the curse of sin surrounds you, still you remain as pure as a lily, even more than all others."*

The bride of Christ still has much to learn in this season of life. She is still immature and self-centered. The cross has not fully broken her, but her identity is that of a worshiper and a lover of God. The power of love has connected to her heart. Whatever lies ahead, she knows that He loves her and that she is the delight of His heart. What is the King's reply to this revelation of her identity? He affirms her value and beauty by calling her His *"darling companion"* who stands *"out among all the rest. For though the curse of sin surrounds you,"* and in the midst of a world filled with thorns,* *"still you remain as pure as a lily."* He calls us His darling companion, His lily in the valley. Please stop and think about that for a moment. You are so precious to Him that He reached His hands into the thorns and held you to Himself. Jesus tore His hands reaching in to rescue you as you have remained pure.

Beloved, you are the fiancée of Jesus Christ, and there is nothing He would not do for you. Calvary's nails were like thorns ripping His flesh, as He had to find you and hold you to Himself. The thorns speak of the curse of sin upon our world (Gen. 3:18). As a fragrant lily, she spreads her blessings, even in the midst of the curse. Without striving or toiling, she is arrayed in beauty in this fallen world. Jesus said to His troubled disciples, *"Observe how the lilies of the field grow"* (Matt. 6:28, NASB).

Beloved, listen to His words: *"Still you remain as pure as a lily, even more than all others."* Among the maidens of the earth, there is one who longs for purity. In the midst of the curse of this fallen world, the bride longs for the Bridegroom. She is the bride of Christ. The King affirms her value, for there is no one quite like her. There is no one quite like you either. Others have hurt Him, but you have nourished His heart. You are like a pure lily surrounded by thorns.** Lilies harm no one; it is thorns that tear and hurt others. Thorns say, "Keep away," while the lily says, "Come, I am here to please you."

We are not merely to be lilies in a vase, but lilies among thorns. When we begin to understand this, we cry, "But, Lord, I am hurt as I walk among the wolves." "Yes, child," He responds, "but you must be My lamb. Just as I clothed Adam and Eve in lambskin, so I send you out as My lamb in the midst of wolves." The darling lily of Jesus will not retaliate. Beloved, it is the ungodly and hurtful who truly teach us to be His lamb, His lily. Is your influence sweet

---

* The curse of sin is like the thorn bush from which God spoke to Moses. In the midst of the thorns of our fleshly life, God would place fire within the heart of His passionate ones, much like He did with Moses.

** Thorns are a picture of the curse of sin. Jesus said that thorns are also those things that choke the seed and keep it from bearing fruit (Matt. 13:26).

in this world? Or are you rough and stern like a thorn bush? May we be those who walk as lilies/lambs in the midst of a world of hurt and abuse. "Lord, make us charming lilies for You, just like You were a lily among the thorns of this fallen world!"

> **My beloved is to me**
> **the most fragrant apple tree—**
> **he stands above the sons of men.**
> **Sitting under his grace-shadow,**
> **I blossom in his shade,**
> **enjoying the sweet taste of his pleasant, delicious fruit,**
> **resting with delight where his glory never fades. (2:3)**

Jesus is sweet to the taste and pleasant to the eyes. Jesus Christ is our tree of life. To know Him is more satisfying than any other relationship we could ever have. In all of humanity, He is the one who fulfills our deepest longings. Jesus alone supplies the needs of our hearts, for He excels them all. At this point, the maiden realizes there is no equal on earth to this King. No one could ever take His place. She is devoted to Him alone, for He is the tree of heavenly fruit. What refreshing He brings to her spirit.

"He stands above the sons of men." When Jesus healed a blind man, his first glimpse of sight was of men walking as trees. Jesus is the tree that *"stands above the sons of men,"* and He alone must fill our vision. Not Paul nor Peter, and neither our favorite prophet, pastor, or teacher. Among all the finest men stands a tree, one more glorious and charming than all the rest. His name is Jesus. He must be our Lover among the young men (gifted ones in the body).

"Sitting under his grace-shadow, I blossom in his shade." The Shulamite has found His voice to be a refreshing voice, and she loves to sit in the grace-shadow that causes her to blossom, to blossom in His shade. It brings her hope like nothing else ever could. Perhaps your father or mother told you that you were worthless, or an ex-spouse cursed you with his or her anger. Nevertheless,

there is a tall and stalwart apple tree among the sons of men that excels them all. Over all the barren trees that have tried to rob you of hope, Jesus is your tree of life.

"Enjoying the sweet taste of his pleasant, delicious fruit." To draw from Jesus's life is to taste the nectar of sweetness. Nothing compares to the fruit of His character, which Paul called the "fruit of the Spirit" (Gal. 5:22–23). These introductory experiences of grace have brought true spiritual pleasure to the Shulamite. She is relating to Jesus under the apple tree, receiving all the fruits of His work for her. What can compare to this? Intimacy with Jesus has completely consumed her. Even a little touch of this will go a long way in growing us up in God. She doesn't stand in *her* shade as she eats; she must dwell in *His* shade to discover these fruits. He is preparing her to step out of her self-absorbed thinking.

"Resting with delight where his glory never fades." How can you describe the pleasure of His presence? It is a "delight" to be near Him, to be safe under His shadow, to rest in shady grace. It is under this shade tree that the human heart finds absolute tranquility. No other resting place gives you true peace like what you experience beneath His shade, *"where his glory never fades."* Humbly, we submit our souls to His authority, and our striving is over.

Under the systems of her angry brothers, she found no rest. Busy with tending the vineyards of others left her discouraged, wounded, and weary. Now she dwells in the secret place of His presence, resting under His lordship, *"where his glory never fades."* Imagine that if the shadow of Peter brought healing, what would dwelling in His shadow do for you? It is impossible to exaggerate how great your eternal Groom really is. Worship becomes a wonder sitting in His shade.

The cross is the tree of life extending its shade to the weary. Finding a resting place beneath the cross where the glory is, has kept the maiden safe and satisfied. She relates to Him on the basis of His work, not her maturity. Why would you want to relate to God on the basis of *your* victory or *your* maturity? When you have a good week, it is His grace that kept you faithful. When you have a bad week, your unworthiness is not the basis of your relationship with God. Feed your heart under the apple tree. Take a nap from striving, until you say, "I rest *'with delight'* in the place *'where his glory never fades.'*"

Pray this prayer today: "I am overwhelmed by Your love for me, Lord Jesus. You call me Your rose, Your lily. Make my life a beautiful expression of Your great love. I am more than a conqueror through the love You have toward me. I give my heart to You and all that I am. I am secure in Your love. Amen."

CHAPTER 10

THE HOUSE OF WINE

**Suddenly, he transported me into his house of wine—
he looked upon me with his unrelenting love divine. (2:4)**

A s the Shulamite sits under the apple tree, she has a vision. Many versions of the Bible translate it as "banquet hall," but in the Hebrew it is actually "the house of wine." She sees the King taking her *"into his house of wine."* As we delight ourselves in God's presence, He invites us even nearer to His heart, into His house of wine. In the first chapter she was taken into the King's chamber, but now she is escorted into His house of wine for the engagement party. Like a joyous host who wishes to entertain his guests, the King has made His preparations for the bride. As the guests enjoy the feast, the King offers the Shulamite His arm and beckons her to come in with Him and taste His wine.

This banquet hall pictures the church in jubilation, where we discover what it means to be inebriated with His love. This is the chamber of joy where love waves as a banner. The fruit of the apple tree now leads to the fruit of the vine. For the believer, the house of wine* is that place of experiencing the Holy Spirit. The

---

* At the traditional Jewish betrothal ceremony, the bride and groom drink from the same cup of wine. The banquet hall is where the King proposes to His bride, which is what Jesus did with His disciples at the last supper.

King longs for the bride to know the Holy Spirit's power, so He is taking her into the deeper experiences of the Holy Spirit as she drinks deeply of eternal love.

The *"house of* [the] *wine"* of His Spirit brings the maiden into a new realm. She has never been to a church service like this before. The heavenlies are opened and she receives a foretaste of what their life will be like together. The exotic smells and beautiful décor remind her that she is in another world. Before her is a splendor and radiance she has never seen before. A King of vast wealth has spared nothing to show her His love. What liberty these guests have in the house of wine. Singing, rejoicing, and dancing—everyone seems so happy. Now the bride understands that this is what the kingdom of God is like. Everyone seems so fulfilled in love, for they have been chosen to partake of the heavenly gift.

The King says, "Come, let Me take you to the house of wine." Jesus is the one who takes us further and further into grace. Zeal alone will not bring us in, nor will our maturity bring us where we want to be—the King alone brings us in. It is His work to carry us when we are off the path like a wayward lamb. He will leave the ninety-nine to go after the one who goes astray (Luke 15:3). Often, wayward lambs kick and resist being taken further, until they renew their hearts to the King. The bride is that lamb being carried on His shoulder into the chamber of joy.

The flag over our conquered heart is *"his unrelenting love divine."* The Shulamite leaves one world and enters another. As she steps into the room, the King suddenly turns to His fiancée and says, "Welcome to My world. You are blessed, protected, and covered." Jesus has raised His flag of persistent, all-consuming, unrelenting divine love over her conquered heart. When we discover we don't have to be perfect to be loved, that we are cherished simply because we said yes, then we are changed forever. There is a truth that strengthens us in our weakness. It's the revelation of the love of Jesus for insecure, still-imperfect Christians.

Knowing the past about a person doesn't make us prophetic—calling them into their future does. The question has never been, can we read the history of a man? The question has always been, can we restore the future of a man? Anyone can read the history of a person, but the heart of the Father is to release the unfulfilled destiny of His broken children.

God's thoughts toward you are saturated with extravagant emotions of desire. You are the focus of His unlimited affection. What furious love! What extravagant love! Disappointments no longer matter when you know this love. What others think of you will no longer mar your soul. When we are not appreciated or noticed, we have a foundation beneath us and a banner over us and a flag waving over our conquered heart that says, "Love." This furious love becomes the theme of our lives. No longer a guilt-ridden religion, but a divine love-call heard in the depths of our being! When we are at our weakest, love abides. This is what we carry to the nations. This is what we carry to the broken and the wounded. Omnipotent love has conquered us. We must tell everyone about this love we have experienced in the depths of our soul. His *"unrelenting love divine"* becomes the definition of our life in these three ways:

1. His *"unrelenting look of love divine"* means we have great confidence in God's endless mercy, even in the midst of our failures and weaknesses. Nothing can shake that confidence when we see His look of love toward us.

2. His *"unrelenting look of love divine"* demonstrates that God will overrule all of the negative and heartbreaking incidents of our life and make them work for our good. This truth sustains us as we wait for the goodness of God to be seen in everything (Rom. 8:28).

3. His *"unrelenting look of love divine"* means that God's raging love will mean more to us than the pleasures of

sin. Love will give us greater comfort and greater exhilaration than any false and fleeting pleasure with sin.

How does it feel to see Him look at you in that way? What a celebration of love we can bring to the lonely of the world. Jesus is a King beyond belief. He has unveiled Himself to you with a divine love look in the house of the wine of His Spirit, a room filled with unrelenting divine love just for you.

Revive me with your goblet of wine.
Refresh me again with your sweet promises.
Help me and hold me, for I am lovesick!
I am longing for more—
yet how could I take more? (2:5)

The maiden's joy has reached new levels. Unable to take it all in, she says, *"Revive me with your goblet of wine. Refresh me again with your sweet promises. Help me and hold me, for I am lovesick!"* Her cry is to be given a greater capacity to feel and know God's love. Feelings of love can be very intense at times. Our aching, lovesick hearts must have more of Him. We desperately want to feel His embrace, yet sometimes we wonder how we could take more, for we are completely lovesick. This love-wound is designed to ruin us for this world. The affections of the human heart are the most precious possession to God, for there is nothing that He wants more. Jesus died to redeem and thus possess human affections.

What exactly are these spiritual hunger pains that we feel as we ache for more of Him? What causes this lovesickness to be awakened in our hearts? It comes from an awakened hunger that Jesus doesn't immediately satisfy. We get stirred to reach out for Him and possess Him in fullness, but the fullness has yet to be released to answer the groan within. This hunger pain forces us into a deeper pursuit of His presence, of Him. This desperate, agonizing yearning is how God enlarges our hearts to receive yet more of Him.

The Hebrew word for *revive* means "to lean upon," or "to take hold of." The bride is asking to rest in Jesus's strength as she asks for more of the love of God to take hold of her. He will take hold of us and give us as much as we can stand, even more than we can handle. We can only be satisfied and strengthened with further revelations of His love. A lovesick bride will soon arise, filled with longing that cannot be described. Will this love last forever? If only the King promised, she would believe it. She is satisfied with the wine of His presence, but how long will it last? She longs for the promises of grace to continue, the promises of the gospel. The words of Jesus are sweet and refreshing like *"apples of gold in settings of silver"* (Prov. 25:11, NASB). The refreshing promises of Jesus are aptly spoken into our need. She cries, "Sustain me with more of the Spirit and refresh me with more of Jesus."

His left hand cradles my head
while his right hand holds me close.
I am at rest in this love. (2:6)

The left arm is a picture of the invisible, unseen activity of God that sustains us; it is away from our view, out of sight. There are so many things God does for us that we don't see and that we will never realize. We can thank Him for the unseen mercies that sustain us and the sweet manifestations of His touch that move us. How kind is our God! He so often withholds things from us that would harm us. He is at work night and day to hold our heads secure in His love. Our God is so kind. The hands that hold the universe now hold the Shulamite maiden. Who could fear when held by a King like this?

"While his right hand holds me close." The right arm is the manifest works of God that embrace us in ways we can see, feel, and discern. At His right hand are pleasures forevermore (Ps. 16:11), with His mighty right arm of power He touches us in love (Ps. 48:10), and by His right hand there is always victory and triumph (Ps. 98:1). His embracing love is our confidence and our comfort.

This divine embrace is what every lover of Christ desires. It will release sweet feelings of being loved and sweet feelings of loving Him back. It is absolutely mysterious and musical.

Here are the new confessions of faith of the Shulamite. Angry words no longer cling to her soul. The old has gone and the new has come. Speak these words over yourself today:

- I am the rose (2:1).

- I am pure as a lily (2:2).

- My Beloved is to me the most fragrant apple tree—above all others (2:3).

- Sitting under His grace I blossom in His shade (2:3).

- I enjoy the sweet taste of His fruit (2:3).

- He brought me to His house of wine (2:4).

- He looked upon me with His unrelenting love divine (2:4).

- I am lovesick (2:5).

- His left hand cradles my head, while His right hand holds me close (2:6).

So the bride rests her head until iniquity is done away. In this beautiful confidence, she falls asleep in His arms. He is so much more than she ever imagined.

"*I am at rest in this love.*" The Shulamite has now become the true sleeping beauty. Overwhelmed by the power of the Spirit in the house of wine (engagement party) she falls asleep, content in the King's embrace. What kind of sleep is this? Doesn't our King want us to be awake with Him? This is the sleep of dying to our self. The maiden falls into His embrace and into a realm of letting go of what she once presumed she understood.

The bride's sleep imparts understanding and revelation. It is not deadly; rather, it is life-giving. True spiritual ecstasy is a kind of death to self. We are removed so that only He will remain. His beauty is overwhelming and His love is often more than we can take. The Shepherd-King responds to the Shulamite:

**Promise me, brides-to-be,
by the gentle gazelles and delicate deer,
that you'll not disturb my love until she is ready to arise. (2:7)**

The King gazes upon the sleeping beauty as all the guests gather to look at her. The King whispers to His guests, *"Promise me, brides-to-be, by the gentle gazelles and delicate deer, that you'll not disturb my love until she is ready to arise."* Do not disturb her in this sleep of ecstasy; she is in love. Do not prematurely force her to snap out of it and return back to the frenzy of the church. The beauty of the King has enthralled her heart.

Many are jealous when they see another Christian who is in love with Jesus more passionately than them. They want to disturb them, awaken them, and demand that they go out and toil like the rest of the vineyard-keepers. Others may even see you as lazy as you sit at His feet, but the Lord sees you as His very own—and that is all that matters.

The word for *gazelles* in the Hebrew is *shabot*, which is the word used for the armies of God. The Lord has an army of gazelles. Those who truly follow the Lord will be tender of heart, like our Lord Jesus. Gazelles harm no one; they are truly beautiful creatures. So the Lord's armies are comprised of those men and women who are gentle of spirit.

Because fellowship with Jesus is so lovely, the King uses the figure of the loveliest of creatures in exhorting the daughters of Jerusalem to refrain from disturbing the resting bride. Who would want to drive away the beautiful gazelle? Who would want to disturb the bride while she is lost in holy love with Jesus? It is time to rest and find her delight in this divine embrace.

The season will soon change, but for now she must cultivate deep intimacy with her Bridegroom. When we are in this stage of our lives, we are not even aware of what is going on around us. We seem to forget that many are headed for destruction—the nations need the message of life. Meanwhile, we think that we are saved for only one purpose, and that is personal pleasure. Sacrifice, warfare, discipline—those are all strange terms to us when we are sitting under the apple tree enjoying the feast of fellowship.

This self-absorbed stage must eventually give way to the development of true character and maturity. We must be equipped and trained to rule as the coheirs of all things. So the King will soon come to the sleeping Shulamite to call her forward. But is she ready to go?

Pray this prayer today: "Father, I long to be consumed by Your love for me. Thank You for a Bridegroom as wonderful as Jesus. By Your grace prepare me fully to reflect Your glory. Help me today to follow my King and demonstrate His love. Develop me completely into the image and likeness of Jesus Christ. I praise and thank You that you hold me and protect me in all my ways. I love You, Father God. Amen."

CHAPTER 11

TIME TO ARISE

Listen! I hear my lover's voice.
I know it's him coming to me—
leaping with joy over mountains,
skipping in love over the hills that separate us,
to come to me. (2:8)

Now it is time to see the Bridegroom in a new light. Jesus has many faces, many expressions of Himself. He is the Lion and the Lamb, the Alpha and Omega, the Bridegroom and the Judge. He is transcendent, infinitely higher than our highest thought of Him. About the time we think we have Jesus figured out, He appears in a way we do not expect. The maiden has so much to learn about this Shepherd-King—and so do we.

Sweet apples, sitting under the shade tree, the house of wine, the banner of love, and being wooed by the Son of God—life is really happening for the Shulamite. Things are great. Spending time with this soul-satisfying Savior named Jesus—what could be better? She has seen His affection for her; she has felt the exhilaration of His love. But for her, Jesus is still the means, not the end. She is in this for her. Most of her declarations still have *her* as the theme, not Him. It is as though He exists only for *her* pleasure. There is much yet for her to learn, so much more!

Jesus wants a mature partner, not just a girlfriend. He desires to have a marriage, not a date. We must be prepared to sit with Him on His throne. Our compromises will have to go, our limited understanding must be enlarged, and our knowledge of Him must increase. The King patiently leads her from one test to the next, equipping her in perfect love.

She will need to remember His unrelenting love throughout all the tests that come her way. The law of her new life will be love. This is a love that disciplines us and changes us, a love that matures us and makes us more like Him. But the rest of her journey will describe the answer to her prayer: *"Draw me into your heart and lead me out. We will run away together—into your cloud-filled chamber"* (1:4). Now He comes to invite her to run with Him as a new season begins in her journey. Ready or not, here He comes.

He is the searching one, looking for His beloved. First she hears His voice, and then she sees His power. He is awakening her by His voice…or is it His song? She recognizes the voice of her Beloved. Others may tell her many things, but it is only the voice of the Beloved that will pierce her inner ear. Jesus comes to her with an entirely new look. It is time for her to see Him in a new dimension.

In her amazement, we hear the Shulamite exclaim, "Look! Here He comes, leaping over the mountaintops. Wow, I have never seen Him do this before. My Beloved, what are You doing on the mountains? I thought You liked shade trees and feeding me on Your promises, Your apples?" She is stirred by the voice of her leaping Prince who is returning in strength and beauty. Who is this who jumps effortlessly over the mountains, bounding over the hills? He is so much more than she ever dreamed Him to be.

Jesus Christ is the leaping Lord of glory! Mountains, hills, barriers, and obstacles—they are all nothing to Him. He knows nothing of discouragement or difficulty. So strong is His love for her, nothing can hold Him back. He will effortlessly leap with joy over the mountains of her unbelief, skipping over the hills of her struggles as though they were nothing. With His voice of power, He can speak to the mountains and they will be removed.

This is not merely the sweet Savior coming to her; this is the sovereign King who lets nothing stand in His way. How energetic and agile He is. How mighty and regal! This Warrior-King is totally victorious and cannot be intimidated by her difficulties (mountains and hills).

What hinders her is nothing to Him. Jesus wants to show her His omnipotent resurrection power, for only God could leap over mountaintops. Mountains of adversity are nothing to your Beloved. He will come, no matter where you are, and sweep you off your feet. He skips with love over all the plans the enemy has designed to hinder you. He leaps over every obstacle with ease. He is the resurrected, sovereign King over all the nations.

He comes to the maiden to lead her to the mountaintops. But will she go with Him? Is she ready to pay the price? It is time for the bride to leave the cozy corner under the shade tree. The leaping Lord will come to challenge our comfort zone and beckon us to come away in sacrificial service. Jesus wants a mountain-leaping partner. He has an agenda to fulfill. The nations must be won and discipled by the King.

Jesus calls us to a life that is risky, inconvenient, and self-sacrificing. We must be His partners in going to the nations, running together on the hills. We cannot just love Him from a distance; we must have a history of running together in resurrection power. It is time to realize that we are not in this just for our own spiritual pleasure.

The bride has responded to the tender affections of God and is in the right place at the right time. The King has her right where He wants her. Enjoying the presence of the Lord and basking in this wonderful experience, she has no idea that the Lord is about to come and disrupt her little spiritual haven. She is still in spiritual infancy and the Lord has every intention to bring her into spiritual maturity, living for *His* pleasure.

It is good to learn the sweetness of communion, but now we must receive power for service. A fierce struggle of spiritual warfare is all around us, and it will require a brave, courageous bride who is willing to go to the mountains with her Beloved.

Let me describe him:
he is graceful as a gazelle—
swift as a wild stag.
Now he comes closer,
even to the places where I hide.
Now he gazes into my soul,
peering through the portal
as he blossoms within my heart. (2:9)

The gazelle is swift and sure-footed, walking on high places. This is a new revelation of Jesus to the bride. The inscription of Psalm 22 reads, "To the Doe (Gazelle) of the morning." This speaks of Christ's resurrection. Jesus is the gazelle who leaped out of the dark tomb on resurrection morning; He skips in resurrection power. The maiden begins to recognize His strength and agility to overcome every obstacle. He is coming to bid her to arise and go with Him in that same power. Jesus loves you so much that He will climb mountains just to be with you, even a mountain called Calvary. This truly is love.

"Now he comes closer, even to the places where I hide. Now he gazes into my soul, peering through the portal as he blossoms within my heart." Jesus comes closer, looking into the house in which the maiden sits undisturbed. For the first time there is a wall between her and her Lord. She now sees that she is not as close to Him as she once thought. She is hiding, and He gazes into her soul. He is out on the mountains and hills, skipping in love and freedom in His eternal triumph. Her wall of self-protection has become her wall of hiding,* which is the same picture as described in Revelation 3:20 where Jesus is outside the door of the Laodicean church knocking, waiting to come in.

---

* The ceremonial law is called a *"wall of partition"* (Eph. 2:14), and a *"veil"* (2 Cor. 3:13). But it was Christ standing behind that wall, waiting and ready to be the Bridegroom to both Jew and Gentile.

When we put up walls to protect us from pain, we are actually shutting ourselves off from the presence of the healer. But even our well-constructed hiding places will not hinder Him. He will come and stand outside, waiting for us to yield to Him (Ps. 18:29). In this new season of maturing love, the bride will be challenged to leave her hiding places to run with Him. And when we hide, we only see what is inward. Seeing our self only causes us to retreat even deeper. We begin to notice inside of us all the things that shut Him out and have kept us from sacred intimacy with Jesus.

"Now he gazes into my soul, peering through the portal as he blossoms within my heart." Jesus looks into me and sees right through me, through the portal of my soul and into all the hidden places, yet He is still patient and kind in all His ways. His love is a window through which He sees us as we really are—truly in love with Him. Can't you see Jesus gazing on His bride? He stands waiting for us to come out. *"Peering through the portal as he blossoms within her heart,"* He looks into her eyes (windows to the soul) and sees that she loves Him, even though she is not yet ready to leave her comfort zone. She wants to hide and make sure she is safe.

As we will see, she says no. He can see it in her eyes. He can hear her thoughts: "I'm afraid of mountain climbing. I am not yet ready. Let me stay here for a while under the shade of Your apple tree. I'm happy here. I'm satisfied. Can't we just sit here together and enjoy one another? Let someone else leap on the mountains and go to the nations. I'll just linger here with You."

Pray this prayer today: "Lord Jesus, I don't want to remain where I am any longer. I promised that if You would draw me close to Your heart, then I would run with You. My day of running with You has come. I want to arise and go into the future holding Your hand and strengthened by grace. Help me to arise and leave my comfort zone behind. You are enough for me. Amen."

CHAPTER 12

LOVE CALLS HER HIGHER

The one I love calls to me:
Arise, my dearest. Hurry, my darling.
Come along with me!
I have come as you have asked
to draw you to my heart and lead you out.
For now is the time, my beautiful one. (2:10)

Every time Jesus speaks to the Shulamite, it is with tender love and affection. How we wish all of God's servants could follow in our Shepherd's example. He calls her His dearest, His darling. Yet there is hesitancy in her eyes as He peers into her heart. What is it that makes her lovely to Him? Jesus acknowledges the virtues that are only budding within her. He will never close His heart to her. Never.

God does not define your life by the 10 percent of you that you hold back from Him, but by the 90 percent of your heart that longs for Him continually. Aren't you glad He defines you in this way? Your weakness is covered by the torrent of His love. He doesn't say, "Why, you hypocrite? You only *think* you love Me. What is this hesitancy I see in your eyes? You are so stubborn and incomplete in your devotion to Me? Your fear and sin makes you ugly."

You will never hear words like that from your Beloved. Even in your failures He holds you fast. He calls you His dearest long before you see His beauty forming in your life. He calls you His darling long before you feel that you are close to Him. You are safe with a King like this. Jesus's love is what imparts the strength to arise and come away with Him. His fiery love has power to break off every desire for the world and its artificial pleasures. His love will consume every other ambition and passion. How can we cling to our dust when He bids us, "Arise"?

Our Beloved would not have us spiritually asleep while nature is all around us, awakening us from winter's rest. He calls me darling and bids me, "Arise." He is risen and I am risen in Him, so from lower loves, lower desires, and lower pursuits I would rise toward Him. "Come away." Further and further from everything selfish, everything worldly and sinful, He calls me; even from the religion of the outward and external, which has no mystery of the higher life. *"Come along"* has no harsh sound in it to my ear, for what is there to hold me in this wilderness of vanity and sin? "O, raise me, draw me. Send Your Holy Spirit to kindle sacred flames of love in my heart, and I will continue to rise and follow You."

If He calls me His darling, if He counts me fair and worthy of being His love partner, who am I to hold back behind my wall? How can I linger among the tents of Kedar when He calls me to the mountaintops? "Come along with Me. Come along further and further with Me. Come along, away from everything selfish and sinful. Come along with Me and leave the religious systems and structures of men to be My bridal partner. Come along into the mystery of higher life in the Spirit. Come along with Me."

This message has no harsh sound to my ear. What could hold me back in this wilderness? To come along with Him is to come home from exile, to come to the shore away from the raging storm, to come to strength and shelter out of my place of weakness. We must be those who pray: "Lord, send Your mighty Spirit to kindle fresh fires of love in my heart until I leave this place of hiding and come along with You."

Beloved one, this is not the time to be hiding behind your wall; this is the time to be learning the ways of the leaping Lord Jesus. It is time to leave the predictable things behind and launch out into the undiscovered country of end-time ministry. Jesus is ready for action. Comforts and human securities must be abandoned as we leave for the high place. We are to be carried by love to a higher place, a greener pasture, a quieter stream. We have not seen it all yet.

When Jesus speaks the word "Arise," He causes the lame to walk. The words of Jesus release the power to perform. In this invitation to arise, the Lord is promising her (and you and me) that there He will give the power freely to take up our bed that once confined us and walk in the power of a new life. Even though we see ourselves as lame and powerless, Jesus can lift us with a word. It is time to arise and shine, for our light has come (Isa. 60:1).

But the maiden is afraid of heights; she doesn't like the mountains. She prefers the couch, resting behind her walls, being fed with apples, and staying safe in her comfort zone. He wants her to walk on mountains; she prefers the couch. She is not yet ready to go. Sound familiar? What are the things that hold us back from pursuing Jesus? The risks of walking in faith! Jesus requires that we risk all in our walk of faith. The voice of the Lord once said to me, "Brian, I have not called you to play it safe." The wild frontier is unpredictable and untamed, but this is where we must go to get to our Promised Land.

Bold faith is always the way of God's kingdom, operating in the confidence of invisible things (2 Cor. 5:7; 4:18). Risky? Yes, but we honor God every time we trust in His integrity. It is a mysterious way to run a kingdom, but this is God's chosen way of drawing us into true devotion to Him. We will not grow until we venture out from our comfort zone and encounter Him in a place of weakness and trust.

Arise, my dearest. Hurry, my darling." No one has ever spoken to the bride in this way, with such tenderness. He enjoys her as His darling while she is still growing, not after she is mature. She has not even said yes to His invitation, yet she is still His beautiful darling. Let this truth wash over you again: Jesus enjoys the immature believer. As a father enjoys his growing child, so the Father enjoys you from the moment your heart said yes to Him. The Shulamite is still behind her wall on the couch hiding from Him, but He knows what is in her heart and He knows what love He has for her.

Jesus calls her beautiful while she is in the process of growing in mature love. A loving father enjoys his child during the messy stages of his or her life. Immature and clumsy, unable to clean up after himself—but he is still loved by his dad. So it is with our heavenly Father—there is no mess He will not clean up for His children. Only believe and walk forward into the fire of His love. We arise out of our negatives and run into His loving embrace. This is the joy of His heart, to see us arise and come away.

The Bridegroom-King enjoys the responsive heart of love. He is not hung up over the particular stage of maturity we are in. God knew we would linger in immaturity when He called us. But given enough time, immature love will bud and grow into maturity. Remember, at each stage of our growth Jesus calls us. So He comes and He says, *"I have come as you have asked to draw you to my heart and lead you out. For now is the time, my beautiful one."*

The King now gives her eight prophetic signs of the new life He is calling her to. A spiritual springtime has now come. He's sharing these secrets with her so that she will arise and come with Him. These words are meant to assure her of His power and of the approaching harvest. These eight statements are meant to stir her heart to arise and come away, for the season has changed and now it is time to experience resurrection life.

**The season has changed,
the bondage of your barren winter has ended,
and the season of hiding is over and gone.
The rains have soaked the earth
and left it bright with blossoming flowers.**

The season for pruning the vines has arrived.
I hear the cooing of doves in our land,
tilling the air with songs to awaken you and guide you forth.
Can you not discern this new day of destiny
breaking forth around you?
The early signs of my purposes and plans are bursting forth.
The budding vines of new life are now blooming everywhere.
The fragrance of their flowers whispers:
"There is change in the air." (2:11–13)

First, *"the season has changed, the bondage of your barren winter has ended."* The chill of a gloomy and angry winter is past. The cold winds of trials no longer blow. If He was faithful during the winter of discontent, then the Bridegroom will be faithful in the springtime of budding grace. The warmth of love has come with new hope. Jesus asks, "Why are you afraid? I took you through the winter, and we are still together. I will take you into the spring. My banner over you is love and My love will see you through!" The kindness of Jesus in our winter season assures us that we will be safe in the springtime of dawning purpose.

During the winter season, all activity is happening below the surface. It is a time of dormancy, with no visible fruit seen by the eye. But when the Bridegroom awakens our hearts, this period of dormancy is over and we enter into the springtime of divine romance. An explosion of new growth and fruitfulness takes place, for the winter is past.

Second, the *"rains have soaked the earth."* The earth is no longer dry and dusty. The Word of God has come and brought pools of refreshing to ready us for the harvest. The rains have readied the earth for new growth, for the flowers and the blossoming vines. All of nature is responsive to the return of spring, but will she respond to His love and run away with Him?

Third, *"and left it bright with blossoming flowers."* Wherever there is a flower, fruit is not far behind. If ever you have felt like your "flower" has faded or fallen, this is good news, for new life is about to come forth. Flowers appear on the vine just before the fruit is harvested. The flowers are prophetic signs of a soon-to-come harvest. It is clear that the "flowers of revival" are budding across the nations. The King is urging her not to remain an immature girl when He needs a mature partner to harvest the nations with the gospel.

There is urgency in His voice here—she must make herself ready as destiny breaks forth on the earth. As flowers blossom all around her, there is no time to waste in joining her King in His mission. Her destiny is on the horizon.

The fourth prophetic sign is that the *"season of pruning the vines has come."* Vines are pruned as the season changes from winter to spring. The season of pruning vines implies the dead growth of the winter is left behind for the budding of the new season to come. God is confidently at work to prune from our lives what has held us back in the winter seasons we pass through.

But we find an amazing secret in the Hebrew text. The homonymic word *zamir* can be translated in two ways. It can be either "singing" or "pruning." Perhaps our songs of worship actually prune our lives of dead things, lifeless matters that hinder our relationship with God. When God prunes us, He sings, for He knows that eliminating "dead branches" from His tree will bring forth an even sweeter fruit of righteousness in us.

"I hear the cooing of doves in our land" is the fifth prophetic sign given to us. This spiritual spring brings the soothing messages of love to our souls; it is like the cooing of doves. The dove has come to sing to our spirits and awaken us in bridal affection for the Son. As this cooing touches our hearts, we arise and prepare ourselves for His approach. We are told that the doves sing at harvest time. If you listen carefully today, you will hear the

cooing of doves in our land.* His kingdom of love is coming to the earth.

Sixth, *"filling the air with songs to awaken and guide you forth"* means there is a time of celebration that is breaking forth. You may have just passed through a season where you had no joy and you were so crushed that you could not sing. Yet, the Holy Spirit is here to announce a season shift has come. The springtime of favor will be discerned by a season of singing.

In Isaiah 54:1–3, the barren woman is commanded to sing even before she gives birth. The power of prophetic song prepares hearts for harvest. The new thing God is unfolding will require new songs to be sung. The season of singing and dancing is here. The singing has begun as houses of prayer are rising up world-wide and as days of worship (Global Day of Prayer, The Call, etc.) gather multitudes to stadiums to sing. How could you hold back when Jesus sings His Song of Songs over you?

Seventh, *"Can you not discern the new day of destiny breaking forth around you?"* A new song is released in our hearts; the break-through is close at hand. Our unbelief has held us back, but no more for our eyes are illuminated and a new realm opens to us. We begin to see what has always been there, but invisible to us because of our fear and unbelief. It's a new day to see what God has prepared for His lover-friends. It's time to see the angel armies surrounding us, ushering us into the new day: *"And Elisha prayed, 'Open his eyes, Lord, so that he may see.' Then the Lord opened the ser-vant's eyes and he looked and saw the hills full of horses and chariots of fire all around Elisha"* (2 Kings 6:17, NIV).

The eighth and final prophetic sign is that the *"budding vines of new life are now blooming everywhere."* This speaks of the thriving grace of God that is upon us, for "the budding vines" are releas-ing the scent of spring. The visible signs of future fruitfulness

---

* How good of God to call it "our land." The Bridegroom has already become one with us. The divine partnership is beginning to emerge. It is our land—not merely something He owns, but something He loves. The two will become one.

are upon us as Jesus sees His bride as a vine covered with buds and blossoms. The fragrance of tender grapes is starting to come forth. The Bridegroom calls His fiancée to share His joy in these fragrant tokens of heavenly life that are springing forth.

"There is change in the air."
Arise, my love, my beautiful companion,
and run with me to the higher place.
For now is the time to arise and come away with me. (2:13)

As the bride-to-be hesitates, the Bridegroom repeats His invitation to come away and run with her King. She must leave herself behind and follow Him in resurrection power as they skip over mountains together. He urges her to step out in faith and prepare for the end-time harvest. The power of the book of Acts is about to be released for the bride in end-time power. An "Acts 29" church is going to arise, and you are going to be needed for leadership in His glorious outpouring.

The Shulamite has so much yet to learn. Jesus is telling her: "Can't you see all the signs of the harvest? Don't draw back now. I want you with Me on the mountaintops." He woos her with bridal love. With no threats, only love, He draws her forward. This is ever the way of our heavenly Bridegroom. Jesus will consistently motivate us with affirmation and grace, not fear and condemnation. Love lifts us higher, much higher than fear of rejection, but we must respond.

Pray this prayer today: "My Lord Jesus, take away every fear that will hinder my love for You. I place all my anxieties and worries at Your feet. You are the Prince of Peace and I cling to You. Let every difficulty shrink as I stand next to You. Thank You for Your glorious peace. Amen."

CHAPTER 13

"EMBRACED IN HER WEAKNESS

**For you are my dove, hidden in the split-open rock.
It was I who took you and hid you up high
in the secret stairway of the sky.
Let me see your radiant face and hear your sweet voice.
How beautiful your eyes of worship
and lovely your voice in prayer. (2:14)**

The Bridegroom can see it in the Shulamite's eyes—she's not going to leave her comfort zone. She can't do it. Like Peter, He could tell her that she is going to betray His love and stay behind. Yet in her weak moment, struggling with fear, He reveals His tender heart of affection toward her. It would be hard to find in Scripture a more powerful statement of the heart of Jesus toward weak, fearful, and immature believers than right here. In fact, He calls her *"my dove."*

The King has heard her worship, her meditation, and it has gripped His heart. He has noticed her beauty. Now He locks eyes with hers and says, "Your passionate eyes are like loyal, gentle doves." He sees in her a beautiful creature that can fly into His heart and abide there forever. The one who has the Spirit without measure is able to see this same Spirit-life in His bride. Who is it that made her eyes like doves, if it wasn't Him? Love makes what is uniquely His available to her.

The eyes speak of the ability to see spiritual truths. She is growing in her perception of who He is. With eyes of faith and clear spiritual vision, she is starting to see how awesome this King really is. We are told that the eyes of a dove are only able to focus on one thing at a time. He sees that she is looking only to Him (Matt. 6:22). She has become single-minded in grace, not tossed about by condemnation and rejection. Her emotional tank is being filled with His love. She is able to see clearly all that He has done for her, as her focus turns to Him alone. Her eyes search for the source of fire that passes through her when He looks at her.

She trusts Him…at least she trusts Him as far as she knows Him. She is learning much, but the great revelation of who He really is awaits her on the mountaintops. But is she willing to go? Does she trust Him enough to go to the mountains of myrrh?

This is a wonderful season in the maiden's life. She is seeing this Shepherd-King as the one who is feeding her apples, embracing her in His arms. Life just doesn't get much better than this. When the Lord comes to you with waves of refreshing, you simply sit back and receive them. Drink in the wine of His love, for you will need it for the lessons He has in store for you—those unexpected lessons He is preparing for you to learn from.

Embraced in her weakness, the Bridegroom describes His love for her as David wrote in Psalm 68:13: *"When you sleep between sharpened stakes I see you sparkling like silver and glistening like gold, covered by the beautiful wings of a dove."* Even the sleeping bride shines with glory in the eyes of our Beloved. We are His pet doves: *"Lord, aren't we your beloved dove that praises you? Protect us from these wild beasts that want to harm us"* (Ps. 74:19).

The dove is a bird that speaks of purity, innocence, peace, and loyalty. A dove never mates again after its partner dies. The Lord affirms to the Shulamite that she belongs to Him and that she will never be content unless they are running together. The loyal dove is the term He uses to describe her—not a snake or a wolf, but His pet dove. His heart is ever reaching toward her even as she hides in fear. Each statement from His heart tells her that He is safe and that He can be trusted.

Jesus had dove's eyes. He ever looked to His Father, single-focused, His gaze always fixed on Him. Jesus was sent by that look of love. Humbly, Jesus left heaven and came to find another who had dove's eyes—a beautiful bride who would see the Father the way He sees the Father.

"Hidden in the split-open rock. It was I who took you and hid you up high in the secret stairway of the sky." What an unusual place to find a dove. An eagle perhaps would fly to the high place, but how did this dove get there? Jesus sees His bride-to-be as a precious dove hidden in the split-open rock, the clefts of the rock. She is nestled in the secret place of the stairs, safe in the hiding place of His love. He has made for her a nest, a dwelling place on high.

The *"secret stairway of the sky"* speaks of the mystery of Jesus's resurrection. It is the ultimate secret place in which a Man ascended to God. The cliff ascends upward as the stairway up to heaven, much like Jacob's ladder (Gen. 28:12–17). *"The secret stairway of the sky"* could also be translated as *"the secret place of the stairs"* (KJV) or *"the secret place of the steep pathway"* (NASB).

Within the wounded side of her Lord, all is safe and secure. The Shulamite was made to soar with Him as His partner for life. It is time to leave the nest and fly with Him over the mountain-tops. Jesus calls each of us to come and fly with Him from the secret place as we go together to the nations with the message of love, the cooing of doves.

Moses was hidden in the clefts of the rock while the glory of God passed by. This was a foreshadowing of our redemption that was to come in Christ Jesus. Moses hiding in the clefts of the rock was a type of salvation through the cross. Jesus is the rock that was pierced for us (1 Cor. 10:4). Nestled in His wounded side, we find shelter from the blazing holiness of God that would destroy us in our sins. Jesus sees the maiden as one who is hidden in the cross. His wounds are our hiding place. Our true life is here in this hidden nest on high (Col. 3:1–4). Fully identified with the cross of Jesus, with no wall of self-protection—this is how Jesus views us. As the Shulamite takes her place in the split-open rock, the things of self and flesh are broken to pieces. Here she will receive heavenly vision and spiritual sight. This rock must be her stronghold and dwelling place. United to the cross, she can live above the circumstances of life with its pain and testing. There will be water gushing from this rock, which will satisfy her and wash her from all defilement. Present here is the call of the cross—to live in the nest as one crucified and raised again to sit on high.

The words used here are actually "in the secret place of the stairs." There is an ascending life awaiting her. Jesus is her "stairway," the heavenly escalator that Jacob dreamed about (Gen. 28:12; John 1:51). This secret stairway is the place of mystery. The maiden has not understood the mysteries of God nor the ascended life. Jesus Christ is clearly the ladder that reaches from earth (His human nature) to heaven (His heavenly nature). Jesus spoke to Nathaniel using the same terminology: *"I tell you the truth, you shall see heaven open, and the angels of God ascending and descending upon the Son of Man"* (John 1:51).

Jacob received the glorious revelation that Jesus is the *stairway* to heaven. By Him we climb the steep pathway and leave this lower life behind. It is when we see Him that the Father speaks to our hearts. All of God's favors come to us on this Jesus-ladder. Jesus is the only valid entry into the spirit realm. He is the way into the heavenlies. Before the Shulamite can be a "sent one" to the nations, she must first see herself as nested in the secret place of the stairs.

Pray this prayer today: "Jesus! You have placed me in Your secret stairway. I am drawing closer and closer to You each day. Thank You for grace that has set me on high. You are a perfect place of peace and rest for me today. In all that I face this day, I trust in You, my shelter and my hiding place. Amen."

CHAPTER 14

YOUR VOICE IS SWEET

Let me see your radiant face and hear your sweet voice.
(2:14)

Now that we are secure in the clefts of the rock, Jesus can freely share His heart with us. He looks at our timid heart and says, *"Let me see your radiant face."* God wants us to run to Him in our weakness, not away from Him in fear. He asks of us: "Let Me gaze into your eyes. Show Me your face." As the Bridegroom looks at the bride in her brokenness, He can see His reflection shining forth. From her place in the hidden stairway, her face is lovely to Him. Instead of hearing a lecture, she is washed in love.

He pleads with her further to look into His eyes: *"Let me see your radiant face and hear your sweet voice."* How her voice moves His heart! He wants to hear her adoring worship and her prayer for help in the coming time of crisis. This is an invitation for the maiden to intercede and cry out to Him, to worship Him even in her place of need. "If only you knew how sweet your voice is from the clefts of the rock," Jesus calls to her. "How lovely you look there hidden in My love. Let Me hear your heart's cry and I will answer you. Your voice is music to My ears—sweet, pleasing, and acceptable to Me."

Instead of her voice sounding repulsive to His heart, her worship and intercession are *"sweet"* to the Lord. May He hear our voice and call it sweet too. There are many voices in this present generation, all clamoring for our attention. There is the voice of human reasoning, the voice of innocent blood, the voice of politicians, and even the voice of the martyrs. However, the one voice that has not yet been heard in its entirety is the voice of the bride. Revelation 18:23 states, *"The light of a lamp will not shine in you any longer; and the voice of the bridegroom and bride will not be heard in you any longer; for your merchants were the great men of the earth, because all the nations were deceived by your sorcery"* (NASB).

"Let me see your radiant face," for it is lovely in My eyes. Jesus loves you like there is no one else to love; He loves you even as the Father loves Him. He is looking into your face and sees love in your eyes. Even though you may feel that you are immature, tentative, and hesitating, you are lovely to the King. He is telling you, "It's time to let Me enjoy you. You have focused on your satisfaction and what I am to you. Now bring your sweetness to My Spirit."

"How beautiful your eyes of worship and lovely your voice in prayer." He is saying to the Shulamite, and He is saying to you and me: "Let Me take pleasure in you." Jesus always finds delight in His times of fellowship with you and me. Can you imagine Jesus looking at you where you are today, and saying, "I enjoy you; I call you delightful; and I love you! Arise from your self-life and let Me break your shackles of introspection and fear that keep you distant from Me. Give Me your worship, for it is sweet"? Just think: Jesus loves your voice in prayer.

> **You must catch the troubling foxes,**
> **those sly little foxes that hinder our relationship.**
> **For they raid our budding vineyard of love**
> **to ruin what I've planted within you.**
> **Will you catch them and remove them for me?**
> **We will do it together. (2:15)**

As we rest with Him in the cleft of the rock, enjoying the comfort of His presence, He is now free to tell us how we can ascend the secret stairway: *"You must catch the troubling foxes, those sly little foxes that hinder our relationship. For they raid our budding vineyard of love to ruin what I've planted within you."* In every love relationship there will be things that hinder love. They can be habits, words, and weaknesses, areas of our lives that will spoil the freshness of love in our hearts. We want to obey Him. We really want to leave our mess and go with Him, but what about the foxes, the compromises, the remaining issues that hinder our spiritual advancement?

He is not addressing the "lions" of rebellion but the subtle areas that seem so minor yet capable of wounding our love for Him. There are no little sins to God. There is no area that is off limits to the Holy Spirit. Everything is significant when the Lord speaks to us about it. Jesus says, *"Will you catch them and remove them for me? We will do it together."* It is a joint project. He will help us and show us where the foxes of compromise hide (Ps. 139:23). Jesus comes to us and says, "It is time for a fox hunt; it is time to remove those areas of darkness in your heart so that the garden within you is not ruined."

Foxes come out at night (hidden areas) and spoil the vines. If unnoticed and ignored, these "little foxes" will destroy the blooming buds of new life. Tie their tails together like Samson did and put the torch of truth to the wood, hay, and stubble of your self-life.

We all have little areas that destroy a life of fruitfulness. They are our "blind spots." Each pocket of compromise must be dealt with. Every entanglement and weight upon our souls must be shaken off so that we can run our race with endurance and swiftness.

Some of the little foxes or *"little folly"* (Eccl. 10:1) that will ruin the inner life are foolishness, pride, slander, anger, laziness, wasting time, worldly thinking, speaking too quickly, defending our self, being touchy or critical toward others, a negative and complaining spirit, impatience, neglect of prayer, exaggeration, self-importance, and an independent spirit. All of these must be thoroughly caught and removed or the budding fruits of new life will be hindered. Remember that foxes are cunning and crafty animals, and so is your flesh life. We catch the lions and the bears but oftentimes miss the foxes.

I know my lover is mine and I have everything in you, for we delight ourselves in each other. (2:16)

"I know my Lover is mine." The bride's sincere love is expressed even in this moment of stumbling. She sees the compromises, she sees His love, and she sees the risks. And she also sees her need. Despite it all she declares that He belongs to her and she belongs to Him. She states her spiritual identity—she knows she is a lover of God. When we struggle we do not cease to be a genuine lover of God, nor do we cease to be loved by God. Our face does not cease to be beautiful to God and our voice in worship does not become offensive to Him.

"And I have everything in you." Jesus's ownership over her heart will eventually be seen in her life. Her heart is His and belongs to Him. Her love for God is expressed in the midst of her stumbling. She does not feel cast aside by the Lord because of her struggle. She is not a hopeless hypocrite. Her confidence is steadfast. She cries, "I know You are mine and that I am Yours. I am not drawing back." She is sincere yet immature.

When we feel failure and are trapped in compromise, this must be our confession: "My Lover is mine, and I am His!" Foxes or no foxes, our Lord Jesus belongs to us in our imperfect condition. This revelation is what will give her confidence in the days to come to catch the little foxes and remove them from her garden.

Her first priority is still to possess Him for her own pleasure. Her love remains immature. She will follow Him as long as where

He leads is pleasing and comfortable. Rather than arising to run away, her thoughts turn to her place of security with Him. Her thoughts are, "You are already mine. Why should I be troubled and have to go to the mysterious mountains to learn more of You? I already belong to You alone. I know where I can find You anytime I want You—feeding among the lilies."

She has yet to experience a true dying to self and brokenness of the outer life. Her own inner satisfaction means more to her at this time than leaping with the Lord on the hills. Yet, even as she speaks, revelation comes to her: *For we delight ourselves in each other.* She begins to understand, "Not only do You belong to me, but I belong to You. You have an inheritance in me, just as I have an inheritance in You. I really do live to serve You."

What a glorious revelation it is when we see ourselves as His! You are the Father's love gift to the Son. You are His heritage, His chosen one, His bride. Jesus gave His sacred blood to purchase your soul. Each crimson drop spilled on the cross speaks of *this* love that made you His.

You are everything He died for, and He will have you fully. He fought for you, defying all the hosts of hell, which made you their prey. He conquered your sins and then He went on to conquer *you* so that you might be His happy captive, His prisoner of hope. You may now say with all your heart: *I have everything in you.* You belong to no other. You do not belong to the world; you live for the world above! You do not even belong to the church—you belong to the Great Shepherd. You do not belong to sin, self, or Satan. You belong exclusively and entirely to the heavenly Bridegroom.

When another comes to try and steal your heart, you may say, "I am already engaged. My Lover is mine, and I am His." Let this sink in: the brightness of God's glory, the Lord Jesus Christ, is all yours. He is yours in His greatness, yours in His sinless and pure life, yours in all that He was, all that He is, and all that He shall ever be. He is not just yours to talk about, or even talk to, but yours to commune with, as a friend. He is yours in every dark moment and every happy day. Yours when you know it and yours when you doubt it. He is yours in His glory—forever yours.

"I know my Lover is mine, and I have everything in you, for we delight ourselves in each other." There are four times in the Song of Songs this phrase is repeated in some form. Her progression of maturity from being self-centered to being God-centered can be seen in how she states this truth. She starts from being only self-conscious and ends up with a mature God-centeredness.

In the beginning stages, her *own* enjoyment of Jesus is her only focus (1:13–14). She talks about what He is *to her* without much awareness of what she is *to Him*. In 2:16 and 6:3, and then finally in 7:10, the bride uses this same language but changes the order to express her concern about what she is *to Jesus*. Jesus is her inheritance. Her initial focus is only upon her spiritual pleasure, which is acceptable to Jesus as a beginning place in the grace of God. Her only focus is that she is loved and has an inheritance in Him. She has little regard at this stage for His inheritance in her.

To take *"delight"* in can also mean to browse among the lilies. This is where you will always find Jesus, among the lilies of His paradise. Jesus loves to find peace among His people of pure heart; they are His lilies. He is refreshed by your loving fellowship. In poetic imagery, we learn the sacred truth that dearest communion with Jesus can never be known by the hard and restless ways of an unbroken heart. This is the priceless heritage of the meek and lowly, those who are like His guarded garden. Like a doe that grazes in a field of white lilies is the Lord of heaven among those with a gentle spirit. He longs to feed us the deep things of His Spirit as we walk with Him in purity.

The inscription of Psalm 45 states that it was written, "To the tune of Lilies." The lilies do not toil, spin, or fear. The Bridegroom calls her His lily. Light is starting to come into her soul. She finds that He really is nothing to fear. He will provide her safety, even on the dark trail leading into the night. She realizes,

"My love can feed His heart…I could become His lily, His place of communion (browsing). He could catch the foxes…we could catch them together."

Yet, even with the dawning of this revelation, she says no. Her focus is still on herself. Her destiny beckons her to come forth, but she is not yet ready. She must endure the pain of His withdrawal to understand what she is missing.

Pray this prayer today: "Lord Jesus, I long to be always at Your side, running with You on the mountains of spice. Help me to overcome every fear that would hold me back. Take away every anxiety from my heart and draw me closer to You. My heart longs for more of You. Increase my desire to go with You wherever You go. I know You will help me, for You are my strength and my Lord. Amen."

CHAPTER 15

HER PAINFUL
REFUSAL

But until the day springs to life
and the shifting shadows of fear disappear,
turn around, my lover, and ascend
to the holy mountains of separation without me.
Until the new day fully dawns,
run on ahead like the graceful gazelle
and skip like the young stag over the mountains of separation.
Go on ahead to the mountain of spices—
I'll come away another time. (2:17)

The Shulamite answers, "No, I cannot go. You go ahead without me. Turn, be like a gazelle on the rugged hills. I am not ready to leave this predictable place to run with You." How painful it is to say no to Jesus. Yet we immediately feel separation anxiety when it appears that He has left us.

The *"mountains of separation"* (or the "hills of Bether") suddenly separate us from our Beloved. We want to say to Him, "You are still my Lover, but I am afraid. Perhaps later, when *'the shifting shadows of fear disappear'* and doubts flee and the full light comes, then I will go." The Shulamite is waiting for another season, not realizing that she is missing the season of running with the King.

She is thinking, "When the day breaks through and fills the sky with light, perhaps *then* I could run with You."

She is not prepared to go with Him. After the cooing of doves is heard, her heart still holds back. She is a reluctant and preoccupied bride. How often does this take place with you and me? We think we need to grow more, to wait until the clouds lift and the darkness flees. We want to see better before we take off into the undiscovered country of growing in Christ. It's hard to walk in the twilight of our immaturity. We tell Jesus to go on ahead without us and leap across the mountains in resurrection strength, for we must grow more. "Go on ahead, Jesus. I'll catch up with You later."

We want the Lord to be with us in our circumstances. We want Jesus present in our pain, when we need Him the most. "Jesus, can't You stay here with me in this cozy, comfortable place behind my wall and make me feel better?" But why aren't we ready to say yes when He needs us to run with Him to the nations? He has plans in His heart for us. How could we say no to His tender affection toward us? We presume that we could do a better job of leading our life than He can. We want to be in charge of our destiny and direct our own path. But true and lasting transformation comes when Jesus is our destiny and our path.

The bride has much to learn. *We* have much to learn. Her mind is set on the future: *"until."* "Someday I'll be His delight and skip with Him on the mountains, but not now. Life is hard and I need to protect myself and hide behind my wall," we say. We must never wait until the imperfections (shadows) flee. Now is the time to arise and run with Him, running out of the shadows and into His glorious light. Our lamps must be trimmed and filled with oil. When we see Him, the shadows have already fled away by the light of His brilliance. The new day has already dawned; the Bridegroom is in the land. As we follow Him, our paths will be like the first rays of dawn that shine more and more until the perfect day shines (Prov. 4:18). The supernatural life awaits you. Will you go?

Upon hearing her words, with His heart breaking Jesus turns away slowly into the night. He leaves her to go up the dark trail— alone. But does He really abandon her? Does Jesus walk away from us when we fail Him? No. Never. He has promised us that He will never leave us or forsake us. He only seems to be distant at times. He lifts from our hearts the awareness of His presence to draw us out to seek Him. He never left the Shulamite; He only walked a few steps away, fading into the darkness, and then He turned around to gaze upon her. Even in our darkness, Jesus is there, present with us, watching and waiting for us to turn away from darkness to find Him in joyful reunion.

Once you have tasted His fruit and held Him in the arms of sacred intimacy, you will never want Him to leave. But Father knows best. God knows just how to mature us through seasons of bountiful blessings and seasons of discipline and dryness. The maiden will learn well the lesson of what happens when we say no to the invitation of Jesus—we are not rejected, but it can be lonely in that self-made wilderness of wanting our own way.

Your King is an amazing teacher. He is faithful to make you over into His image. He is pleased when you begin to show the fruits of His life living through you. To obey is not easy; there is a cost to your obedience. But the cost for disobedience is even greater. God will orchestrate the test for you that will show you the right path. This test will prove to be the easiest trial that will awaken your heart to obey again. Even though difficult, your tests are never greater than the faithfulness of God to keep you and see you through.

Night after night I'm tossing and turning on my bed of travail.
Why did I let him go from me?
How my heart now aches for him,
but he is nowhere to be found! (3:1)

Her refusal to go to the mountains with Jesus brings a sleepless night. She had seen Him turn away to walk alone to the high place. For a season, He is hidden from her. There are times when God strategically hides His face from us so that we look for Him with greater earnestness. He withdraws the *awareness* of His presence to draw our hearts toward Him. This is a form of divine instruction to the soul. It often happens when we need Him the most. We feel vulnerable, forgotten. Our feelings betray us and eventually confusion sets in.

Although we rarely interpret these times as "training," yet it is God's way of disciplining those He dearly loves. Depression often hits us when we no longer feel close to Jesus. He is always there and we know His Word is true, yet we *feel* far from Him. Temptations to return to old habits will intensify during these times of discipline. "Where did He go?" At times, the Devil may try to convince us that God doesn't really care about what is happening to us, and disappointment clings to our soul. We begin to mistake His discipline for rejection, but love is strong, even in the season of discipline. What are we to do in times like these? We must seek Him even in the dark, when we don't feel Him. This is the key that turns darkness to light.

The Shulamite maiden continues to pray on her bed behind her wall of isolation. This is not merely one sleepless night, but a *season* of discipline in her life. This season is a time of darkness and separation for her. She feels the remorse for saying goodbye to the one she loves. How oppressed we can feel in times like these. Seeking Him in our "night seasons" will create desperation in our hearts. It causes us to overcome the natural tendency to sleep (backslide) and push away inconvenience to find our Beloved.

Every believer will one day go through a dark "night" season when there is nothing to cling to but our Lord Jesus. Here are three different "night seasons" in our spiritual life in which we must seek the Lord.

1. The night of pain. In difficult circumstances, as when David ran from Saul and Joseph was in the dungeon,

they did not give up by concluding God's promises were false. In this night of pain, God will often speak to us in a new language—the language of silence.

2. The night of temptation. In times of failure and darkness, we must continue to seek God.

3. The dark night of the soul. This indicates God's presence being temporarily withdrawn in times of obedience (5:6) to test us and draw us out to seek the Lord in greater intensity.

Where is he—my soul's true love? (3:2)

This is the title she gives Jesus: *"my soul's true love."* Her love for Him is strong, even in the night seasons of her life. When confusion and restlessness enters her heart, she still reaches out to find Him. There is no desire more powerful than the longing of a soul to know Jesus.

Love for Jesus will break the power of a thousand sins. Once you have tasted the sweet wine of His love, pursuing Him is all you can do. Have you been touched by an unrelenting passion to hold Him? Your night season has been designed to draw you deeper into Him, until you cry out: *"My soul yearns for you in the night"* (Isa. 26:9, NIV).

Pray this prayer today: "Thank You, God, for every difficult season of my life. You have brought me through each one and made me stronger and more tender toward You. Help me to focus on You and not my problems today. You are the kind Father I've always wanted. Your power and Your Spirit will bring me safely through anything I might face today. My hope is in You. In Jesus' name, amen."

CHAPTER 16

LESSONS FROM THE NIGHT SEASON

So I must rise in search of him,
looking throughout the city,
seeking until I find him.
Even if I have to roam through every street,
nothing will keep me from my search.
Where is he—my soul's true love?
He is nowhere to be found. (3:2)

What are the lessons of the night season that we are to learn? We are led into a deeper honesty, a searching of our hearts for what drove Him from us in the first place. Often there are undiscerned issues—hidden faults that must be discovered—or we will continue to grieve the Holy Spirit. These seasons produce a more sincere humility in us. We are forced to see our weakness and live by faith. No one lives with unbroken feelings of God's presence. We all must lean on Him as our source of godly emotions.

Jesus wants a bride He can show off to the universe, a bride worthy to share His throne. This requires repeated dealings from God to get us to this place. Often it seems we are bruised in life, wondering why God is distant and detached from our pain. But this is all a divine setup to make us desperate for Jesus alone. Someday He will show us off to the entire universe and say of us,

"See what My love has brought forth! Satan has no place in her. I have conquered her fears; I have brought her forth in holy passion to sit with Me on My throne. Father, here is My bride!"

"So I must rise in search of him, looking throughout the city, seeking until I find him." Love for Jesus conquers the maiden's fear of the night. She determines to arise and seek Him—nothing could keep her back now. She disobeyed the command to arise in 2:13 and go to the mountains with Him. Now she understands what it costs her to miss the call of God. We often think of how much it will cost us to obey what He has spoken to our hearts, but we seem to conveniently forget about the cost of disobedience.

Lack of tender response to God costs us more than we could ever imagine. He has chastened the Shulamite by withdrawing the sense of His presence for a season. There are three responses we can have to this discipline. First, we can take it lightly (but He means business); second, we can take it too heavily (but faint not, for He only disciplines those He dearly loves); and third, we can endure the discipline and learn the lesson (He is truly tender and compassionate).

The pain of losing His presence motivates the Shulamite to arise from her bed in the middle of the night and go after Him: *"I must rise in search of him, looking throughout the city, seeking until I find him."* She is incurably devoted to Jesus, unable to live without Him. Is this how you feel when life is difficult? Do you shake off your slumber and seek Him? Or does self-pity keep you bound, causing you to sleep in the midst of your pain?

One of the reasons we do not find Him is because we look for Him in all the wrong places. We are not called to our bed but to the mountains. To look for Him in the place of slumber is to look in the wrong way. She was compelled to get up and go out in search of Him. To "deny ourselves" means we will deny the comforts and ease of pleasing self in order to arise and seek Him alone.

We ache over the distance between where we are and where we want to be. How can we continue to lay here another day in lethargy when He has called us to arise? Yes, it is hard to get up in the middle of the night, but it is much harder to live apart from the sweet communion of being with Jesus (Acts 4:13). The glorious freshness of time with Him cannot be compared to being comfortable behind our wall. Arise, beloved, and search for Him!

The "city" is a picture of the church (Heb. 12:22), and the city of God speaks of the purpose and destiny of God for our lives (Heb. 11:10). The corporate activity of people is in a city ("its streets and squares"). The church, like a city, has government (elders) and order. The Shulamite's desperation for Jesus drives her to involve herself again with others.

We will always find Him in fellowship with His flock, His people. Jesus loves messed up people. To avoid fellowship with other believers is to avoid Him, for He dwells among His people. When our hunger reaches the point where we cannot stand our self-imposed isolation any longer, Jesus brings us into His "city" to reveal Himself to us. There is a risk in moving about in this city. People can harm us and wound us, but this is where we must go to seek Him.

Then I encountered the overseers as they encircled the city.
So I asked them, "Have you found him—my heart's true love?" (3:3)

The watchmen are keepers of the "city" (church). They are the true spiritual shepherds who watch over our souls (Heb. 13:17; Ezek. 3:17; Isa. 62:6). Watchmen are responsible for overseeing the affairs of the city and for watching over that city so enemies do not attack it. The safety of the city (or church) is entrusted to these heaven-sent watchmen. These are the same ones Solomon referred to as "shepherds" in 1:8.

She is now recognizing spiritual authority in the body. They are true spiritual shepherds doing their duty. They find her troubled and distraught as she questions them, *"Have you found him—my heart's true love?"* She had lost His presence; perhaps they could help her find Him once again. She humbles herself before them as she asks for their help.

Our Lord Jesus is serious about issues of spiritual authority and utilizing team ministry. This is how His kingdom operates. Many problems arise when we ignore these truths. So the Shulamite looks to the watchmen, asking, "Have you seen Him?" This is the question sincerely asked to today's shepherds over God's flocks. Leaders are only capable of leading when they have seen Him. Have you seen Him? Do you *know* Him? Is He living in you?

Just as I moved past them, I encountered him.
I found the one I adore! (3:4)

There are times we must go beyond the watchmen in order to find the one we love. Watchmen are a blessing, but they are not Him. We may love the watchmen, those who minister to us, but no one can take His place. Our deepest, fondest, purest love is saved for Him alone, not for those who point the way to Him. When the bride is able to see beyond them, she found *Him!* Jesus suddenly renews His sweet love to her heart. She is thrilled to find Him again. It was worth going out into the dark night to seek for the Beloved. The Lord is faithful and good. He was only waiting for her to come to Him. Love brought her near. Jesus makes Himself easy to find to the seeking soul.

I caught him and fastened myself to him,
refusing to be feeble in my heart again.
Now I'll bring him back to the temple within
where I was given new birth—
into my innermost parts, the place of my conceiving. (3:4)

This is a deeper experience than just finding Him. We must *hold* Him dear. Clinging to Him, the maiden resolves never to let this happen again. The pain of her spiritual darkness taught her a great lesson. How do we hold Him? It is only through the power of holy resolve.

This is what our Lord said in John 15: *"Abide in Me."* Likewise, the disciples on the Emmaus road urged Him strongly to stay with them. We must not only run after Him, but we must hold Him tightly once we have found Him. With Jacob's boldness, we must cling to Him until the shadows flee, as poor sinners holding on to omnipotence.

Have you let Him go? It is comparatively easier to climb the mountain of His presence than it is to stay there. Jesus tells us to abide in Him, to remain with Him each moment, clinging in grace to His hand—this is our goal and our delight. A branch does not come and go; rather, it remains with the vine, connected to its source. Our lives are too filled with moments of letting Him go. Real love will cling to Him, no matter what. Our Beloved is willing to be held. He loves our "sacred violence" that takes Him by force! Faith and love hold Him fast. We are to wrap our golden chains of love around Him, and He will abide with us forever.

The rest of the story is the outworking of holding on to Him. She deeply resolves to never consciously turn her back on Him again. A new zeal enters her spirit to keep Him near her heart. This "holy violence" causes us to prevail (hold on to Him) until we break through our barriers into kingdom living (Matt. 11:12; Gen. 32:26). There are times when God will only respond to us when we have the holy resolution burning within us. Our intense love conquers His heart and He moves to lift us higher in grace. He will not refuse such focused longing. Like Mary did in the garden, when we find Him, we must hold Him tight.

"Now I'll bring Him back to the temple within, where I was given new birth—into my innermost parts, the place of my conceiving." She's done with playing games. She is tired of tossing and turning and done with searching for Him. So she makes a resolution that she will keep Him forever close and will guard her heart, going to that place of first love where she first met Him. She wants to hold on to Him (assimilate His life). Her soul is so in love with Jesus that she cannot possibly live without Him.

The Bridegroom-King says:

Promise me, O Jerusalem maidens,
by the gentle gazelles and delicate deer,
that you'll not disturb my love until she is ready to arise. (3:5)

The King puts a Do Not Disturb sign over her soul and charges the people to leave her alone during this season of renewed intimacy. There are times when we need not trouble the tender souls with fervent serving when they are in a season of sacred intimacy. Often we misread what God is doing with another, as we do not have enough discernment to really know what His plan may be in the life of another individual.

The *"Jerusalem maidens"* are the immature believers who do not understand the various operations of the Spirit of God in the human heart. It is a mistake to disturb them with our premature judgments. Spending time with Jesus and drawing from His life is the very thing that will transform the weakest saint. God is making us into mature coworkers with Jesus who will disciple the nations. This requires times of serenity and times of service. Wisdom knows the difference.

Jesus often needs to remind us not to get in His way with how He deals with His maturing bride. We have human pity and unsanctified mercy for those He is chastening. Those who are in a season of drawing apart, we seem to want them to get back into the rat race of the church. Be careful that you don't distract God's people with your opinions of what God is doing. He takes each of us into different seasons to make us more like Him.

"Until she is ready to arise." He reminds the immature maidens of Jerusalem not to disturb her until she recognizes the new season of the Lord's dealings. *"By the gentle gazelles and delicate deer"* speaks of the need for extra gentleness and sensitivity in relating to those who are immersed in a season of renewed intimacy. They must be allowed to draw near to God without our distractions.

Pray this prayer: "Lord Jesus, I want to have undistracted love. I want to be locked into Your heart and never get out. I long to be covered in Your love and embraced by grace. Stir my heart today to burn with holy love toward You. Amen."

CHAPTER 17

THE CHARIOT
OF LOVE

**Who is this one ascending from the wilderness
in the pillar of the glory cloud?
He is fragrant with the anointing oils of myrrh and frankincense—
more fragrant than all the spices of the merchant. (3:6)**

In this season of increased intimacy, the Shulamite's spiritual eyes opened to see the Lord in a new way. Perhaps in a vision or dream, she hears the Holy Spirit asking her a question: *"Who is this one ascending from the wilderness in the pillar of the glory cloud?"* The wilderness or the desert speaks of life on a fallen planet. Jesus Himself was once driven by the Spirit into the wilderness to be tested by the Devil and proven faithful. Our King came out of the wilderness victorious. After the resurrection, He entered the glory of God, a *"pillar of the glory cloud,"* to sit on His throne.

Can you see the picture of the glorified Jesus rising up from this desert wilderness of earth into the realms of beauty? Pillars of holy smoke transported Him into the temple not made with hands. With the fragrance of myrrh and incense, the King ascends as the ancient doors are opened for the Bridegroom-Savior. Magnificent in His fresh anointing, He now receives the worship of all.

King David in Psalm 24 asked a similar question: "Who is this King of Glory?" Jesus is now a King who is no longer limited to His humanity in the wilderness. Clothed in splendor, He came up out of this fallen world to reenter the glory cloud of heaven. He is *"the pillar of the glory cloud"* that comes up out of the desert.

The glory cloud speaks of the glory and majesty of God on display (Exod. 40:34; Isa. 4:5; 2 Chron. 7:2; Rev. 15:8; Joel 2:28–30). The cloud is the result of the smoke coming from the fire of the Holy Spirit burning up the sacrifices offered to God. The Lord Jesus Christ is coming with the glory clouds to take His seat of honor.

Now the bride has a vision of how marvelous He really is—a wonderful, all-powerful Savior. She will be safe in the desert with Him at her side. Because He conquered His wilderness, so will we conquer ours with Him.

"He is fragrant with the anointing oils of myrrh and frankincense." The ascension of Jesus reveals both His suffering (myrrh) and His splendor (frankincense). As a burial spice, myrrh reminds us of the sacrifice of Jesus to redeem the bride and purify her for Himself. Jesus is perfumed in myrrh. When He was on the cross carrying our sins, He was drenched with myrrh. The sufferings were agony to Him, but they were perfume to the Father. The frankincense speaks of Jesus's intercession for the saints (Heb. 7:25). As Jesus ascended to the Father, He filled the golden bowl of incense with the fragrance of His intercession. What a merciful friend He is!

"More fragrant than all the spices of the merchant." He is more fragrant! What a fragrance that surrounds Jesus, He is always more than any other! He is *"more fragrant than all"* of the sacred spices surrounding Jesus. Who is the merchant referred to here? Jesus is the merchant who saw the pearl and sold all He had to claim the treasure of your love. You are His inheritance, His bride. He bought you as a merchant would purchase the finest pearl. It cost Him His life to make you His bride (Matt. 13:44–46). Sacred blood was shed for you.

Look! It is the king's marriage carriage.
The love seat surrounded by sixty champions,
the mightiest of Israel's host,
are like pillars of protection. (3:7)

"Look! It's the King's marriage carriage. The love seat..." After finding the one she loves, the Shulamite receives the revelation of the King's carriage coming for her. This is actually the Hebrew word for couch, the place of rest and refreshment. In 3:1 she was on her bed of ease, now she rests on His couch of protection. The revelation of this marriage carriage will cast out the fear that kept her from going to the mountains.

The role of the Holy Spirit is to convince us that we are safe with Jesus. Many fear what it would cost to fully live for Jesus, 100 percent. Fear of missing out on the pleasures of life cause many to compromise. This is because we do not know how safe we are in His love. The lies of the enemy will always come with an accusation against Jesus. Can He be trusted? Will He be there? What if He lets me down or disappoints me? The Devil's lies will produce fear in our hearts. Some people do not sever ungodly relationships because of the fear of being alone. Some do not tithe to the local church because they fear they will be left without adequate resources. But fear leads to compromise—always!

The Holy Spirit wants to show us the King's glorious nuptial carriage. This is the wedding carriage, or palanquin, carried on the shoulders of His servants. In ancient times, far eastern brides were carried on men's shoulders in a sedan chair, referred to as a carriage. The bride and groom reclined within the veil, screened by curtains from public view. Bodyguards accompanied them as blazing torches lit up their pathway. This is the picture the Lord would show us of how we are carried through life in His covenant of grace.

We dwell with Him behind curtains. Like the Ark of Covenant, we are hidden with Him, concealed from the world and carried throughout life. Solomon's sumptuous carriage shows us how safe we are in the finished work of the cross where Jesus triumphed over all His foes. There is no safer place than to be with Him in His majestic carriage. Actually, we are carried to the mountains in His gospel couch. If we are destined to sit with Him at His side enthroned as His royal queen (Rev. 19:6–7; Eph. 2:6), then this is our destiny: we will be kept safe in this age as His bride-to-be. The chariot of our Lord Jesus is a cloud of glory.

"Surrounded by sixty champions, the mightiest of Israel's hosts, are like pillars of protection." These warriors are the angels of God that surround us and minister to us (Heb. 1:14). This is extravagant protection. Presidents and statesmen only have twenty to thirty bodyguards around them at any one time—yet you have sixty. Jesus is capable of keeping His bride safe and protected. In the days of Solomon, it was common for wedding parties to be ambushed and robbed, harming the royal family and stealing the gold and jewels. You will not be ambushed by the Devil when you are riding with your King in His royal chariot. Jesus has His noblest warriors surrounding you.

**They are angelic warriors standing ready with swords
to defend the king and his fiancée
from every terror of the night. (3:8)**

None are novices. They are all trained for war and prepared for any difficulty that might come. Intercessors are also like warriors with swords. God has ways of protecting the bride of His Son.

**The king made this mercy seat for himself
out of the finest wood that will not decay. (3:9)**

King Solomon, the King of Israel, is a picture of the Lord Jesus. Jesus made the marriage carriage for Himself. Did you know that Jesus, the Creator, spoke into existence the tree that was fashioned into His cross? By His work on Calvary's cross, Jesus constructed a carriage that would express His love to the entire world. Our resting place is the cross; we are carried along in the safety of His cross.

"The King made this mercy seat...out of the finest wood," means He made us of flesh, as wood is a typology of humanity in Scripture. We are the vessels that carry His glory, created specifically for that purpose. And we were created *"out of the finest wood that will not decay,"* which is a type of the humanity of Jesus. He descended from the ivory palaces (Ps. 45:8) to take on the flesh of man and partake of our human nature (symbolized by the wood). Wood from Lebanon was the most costly and fragrant wood available at the time. Jesus was like us, yet He was also unlike us—He is the greatest of all, the Son of Man. Costly and fragrant was His sacrifice on a wooden cross for us.

> **Pillars of smoke, like silver mist—**
> **a canopy of golden glory dwells above it.**
> **The place where they sit together is sprinkled with crimson.**
> **Love and mercy cover this carriage,**
> **blanketing his tabernacle throne.**
> **The king himself has made it**
> **for those who will become his bride. (3:10)**

"Pillars of smoke, like silver mist—a canopy of golden glory dwells above it." The pillars supporting the covering and curtains were made of smoke—holy smoke. We're covered in God's glory. And the silver mist is the symbol of redemption. Pillars of justice, power, love, and faithfulness provide our covering. And the silver speaks of Jesus Christ, who is our redeemer.

The upholstery *"sprinkled with crimson"* points to the royalty of the Lord Jesus, for a king wears purple. And what a purple this is! It represents the precious blood of Christ that was shed for us over two thousand years ago. We rest enthroned on a scarlet seat of royal authority, a chariot of salvation, because of the blood of Jesus shed on our behalf. Therefore, we can rejoice without fear or doubt in the glory of the cross. Jesus's blood has paid the price.

The carriage is *"covered with love and mercy...for those who will become his bride."* This wedding carriage is meant to be a place of comfort and security even for the immature and incomplete. There is a covering of love and mercy over the Lamb's wife. She is surrounded by priceless love and mercy. Those on the outside cannot fully appreciate what it is to be carried along under this exquisite canopy.

Come and sit side by side with Jesus in His chariot of grace. Be carried with the one who carried your cross. What a soft and pleasant place to recline. Our Bridegroom finds rest in your love, even as you rest in His love. Although there are still many things wrong with the bride, she is carried in the carriage of love and mercy. The affections of Jesus are the foundation of our relationship with Him, not our own feelings. Love brought Jesus to earth. Love led Him to the garden. Love took Him to the cross. And it is love that brings Him to our hearts. Jesus and His fiancée will someday reign together from this crimson throne.

From the finest wood, to silver, to the seat of crimson, the description advances step by step. Each phrase reveals more of the quality and preciousness of our salvation. As we go on with God, we discover more of the astounding glory of our salvation. Filled with new understanding, she exhorts others to gaze at the glory of the King:

Rise up, Zion maidens, brides-to-be!
Come and feast your eyes on this king
as he passes in procession on his way to his wedding. (3:11)

The daughters of Jerusalem are now referred to as the *"Zion maidens."* This is the spiritual term used for the people of God. Now the maiden is seeing the people with eyes of hope and love. Using the same method of encouragement toward the people as the King used with her, she prophesies of their growth in maturity. They will rise up to become the *"Zion maidens"* who love the King. She points their gaze toward Him.

The Shulamites in the last days will always preach Jesus, pointing others to look to Him, not the messengers He sends. There is one with a crown, while all others remove their crowns in His presence. She is saying to the "Shulamites-to-be," the daughters of Jerusalem, the Zion maidens, *Come and feast your eyes on this King.*" Now is the time to crown Him as Lord and join the journey of the bride.

This is the day filled with overwhelming joy— the day of his great gladness. (3:11)

How we underestimate the joy we bring to Jesus. This wedding day is called *"the day of his great gladness."* Nothing thrills the heart of the Son of God like the thought of you! All of heaven is waiting to rejoice together with great joy when He receives us as a bridegroom receives his bride.

Isaiah 62:5 states, *"As a bridegroom rejoices over the bride, so your God will rejoice over you"* (NASB). We are the partners Jesus has longed for. On the day of His wedding, His heart will burst with joy, for He will have you for Himself at last. Make His heart glad today. Worship Him!

Pray this prayer today: "Lord Jesus, I want to please You and enter into the gladness of Your heart. I am Yours and You are mine. Come reveal Yourself to me. I want to see You unveiled in the glory of Your Father. In everything I walk through today, express Your life through me, for You are my life, my all. Amen."

CHAPTER 18

A SACRIFICE READY TO BE OFFERED

Listen, my dearest darling,
you are so beautiful—you are beauty itself to me!
Your eyes glisten with love,
like gentle doves behind your veil.
What devotion I see each time I gaze upon you.
You are like a sacrifice ready to be offered. (4:1)

The romance of heaven is the theme of this inspired story. Jesus has found His princess bride and now He sweeps her off her feet. Like only this King could do, He speaks words of tender love to her, words that wash over her soul, words of unconditional love. He speaks over her (and us) words that inspire and prophesy of her destiny.

As the Bridegroom of our soul, Jesus's love will nourish and sustain us through everything that may come our way. The bride has yet to face the dark night she will soon experience. Knowing what is coming, He now speaks to her the words that will hold her fast in the time of trouble. Drink deeply of the words of your Lover-Friend, O beloved one! You too will need to draw strength through these words during the challenging seasons of life ahead.

Another wave of holy love washes over the bride, a love that will conquer her fear and her mistrust of the King. There is no scolding in the Song of Songs—only affirmation. We see the longing heart of God to be gracious (Isa. 30:18). It is astonishing every time we hear words like, *"Listen, my dearest darling, you are so beautiful."*

Can you see Jesus Christ standing before you this day saying those very words? He knows all about you and me, our stumbles and our tumbles, and still His thoughts are filled with love for each of us (Ps. 139:17–18). He has erased our sins, destroyed the evidence, deleted the files, and washed us squeaky-clean! He refuses to be our probation officer—He is our Savior.

Jesus could bear your sins easier than He could bear your hopelessness. He loves you, He likes you, He adores you. He offered sacred blood to redeem you and make you part of His eternal bride. As His bride, His open heart of love is revealed to you with indescribable joy: *"You are beauty itself to me!"* The very God who created beauty calls His bride to describe beauty when He could have used anything else in all of creation, but here He describes us as *"beauty itself."* What a Bridegroom-King we serve! How could you not love someone like this? No one else would ever describe you in this way.

We need to invent new words to begin to describe God's love. We have a longing Father who waits to see us take one step back into His limitless, liberating love. The love of Jesus is not a temporary mood swing between His acts of judgment. His mercy endures forever. It endures past our failures, our immaturity, and our feeble attempts at walking with God. Our Abba is a friend who calls us beautiful even when we are most aware of our weaknesses. His heart skips a beat when we draw near to Him even when our lives don't seem to work right.

We often see ourselves as shameful and unworthy of His affection. It becomes a mystery why He takes delight in us. It is time to hear Him sing His song of all songs. This is the message that pierces our hearts with mercy. Loved in our immaturity, enjoyed by Him even while we have a hard time living with our self. What a King! What a Friend!

It must be repeated: This is the way God has chosen to change His weak, imperfect bride. He washes her over and over again in cherishing love, removing the stain of sin from her soul (Eph. 5:29). The Holy Spirit will reveal the cherishing ministry of Jesus to the end-time church.

Many are the husbands who try to change their wives in some other way (and the wives who attempt to change their husbands). It is only the power of love that breaks the power of inbred sin. The one who embraces us is stronger than the power of sin in our hearts. His love breaks the stony heart to pieces, making us a responsive, tender bride.

This is how He defines our life: not by our weak stumbles but by our desire to be a delight to Him. Jesus did not define the maiden by her lack of discipline, her heart of fear, and her momentary weakness. He knows the sincere desire in her spirit is to overcome these things and be fully His. He knows what she is becoming, and He knows she will be leaning on Him as she comes up out of the wilderness.

The Bridegroom-King describes the Shulamite by the budding virtues coming forth, not the momentary failures of her life. He can see the awakened passions in our hearts even before they are fully walked out. God called Gideon a "mighty man of valor" while he was hiding in fear of the Midianites. God defines us by what we will be in the future, not by what we are currently doing with our lives. He sees destiny over us and describes us by that. He is a God who calls things forth before they are—this is His job description (1:8, 15, 16; 2:10, 13; 4:1, 7, 10; 6:4, 10; 7:1). Jesus's beauty is reflected by those filled with His love.

End-time ministry in the church must follow the example set forth in this prophetic masterpiece, the Song of Songs. Those entrusted with the care and nurture of the bride must be affirmers, shapers of destiny, encouragers, and lovers of others. Saint-perfecters must be those who focus not on the inabilities and weaknesses of others, but on the budding virtues Jesus is bringing forth within. His *love* gets the job done, not angry exhortations.

Those who cooperate with Jesus in bringing forth the radiant bride will be gripped by the reality of His love. Jesus grows Christians by affirming them, not condemning them. Perhaps we could begin to follow the example of the one who has waited for all eternity for His cherished bride. This is the strongest emotion in the heart of God—Jesus has holy love in His heart for you.

The eight features of the maiden in this passage are pictures of the eight budding virtues that Jesus sees in His bride.* He prophetically affirms her inward beauty with each description of her appearance. Jesus prophesies of the maturity that will arise in her and overcome the accusations of Satan. New creation life is coming forth within her as she becomes His crown of beauty.

"Your eyes glisten with love, like gentle doves behind your veil." Her gentle dove-like eyes refer to the eyes of her understanding (Eph. 1:18). Her heart is open and glistening with love for Him. The Shulamite is "seeing" Him as He really is. The first thing Jesus honors is her perceptive gentle eye of faith. Her supernatural ability to perceive things is a part of her growth into maturity. The enemy seeks to "blind the eyes" of people to keep them from the riches of the gospel that shines in the face of Christ (2 Cor. 4:4). Leah's eyes were "weak," which means she had limited spiritual insight (Gen. 29:17). It is with dove's eyes and eyes of love that the Shulamite maiden gazes on her King (Isa. 17:7).

The dove speaks of purity, loyalty, and devotion.** Her eyes seek purity and look for goodness, not evil. Just as a dove's eyes can only focus on one thing at a time, her heart is single in focusing on Him—there could be none other (Matt. 6:21–23).

"Behind your veil" means that she is concealing her understanding

---

* He gives her a new identity (eight equals new beginning) so she will grow into it.
** The Holy Spirit Himself is seen in Scripture as a dove (Matt. 3:16).

behind the veil of humility. This is always a sign of true spiritual maturity in the saints of God. Many revelations and experiences in God are to grow us in faith and produce Christlikeness within us. To prematurely share these experiences diminishes their power to deeply change us. Paul waited fourteen years before he shared what happened to him in a heavenly experience (2 Cor. 12:1–9). True revelation, covered with humility, equals godly character. We must never take the "pearls" of true spiritual revelation and flippantly share with those who have no heart to receive it. Behind the veil is where the glory dwells. May we have dove's eyes *"behind our veil."*

"What devotion (hair in most translations) *I see each time I gaze upon you. You appear to me like a sacrifice ready to be offered."* A Nazarite was one who was forbidden to cut his hair as an outward sign of his inward dedication to God (Num. 6:1–5). This was a part of a Nazarite's vow of separation to purity. Samson, a Nazarite, had long hair, which was the secret of his strength (Judg. 16:17), and so it is with the bride. A heart fully devoted to God will be strong and mighty for righteousness.

When the King notices her heart yielded in holy devotion, it moves Him. Her long hair is compared to a flock of goats that have descended from Mount Gilead. Gilead was the place where the sheep and goats were kept, awaiting sacrifice in the temple. The sacrificial lambs grazed on Mount Gilead. Jesus extols the bride's dedication, comparing it to a goat coming from the mountain ready for sacrifice. She becomes a *"living sacrifice"* by her response to the mercies of God (Rom. 12:1). Like a dedicated offering is her heart of devotion. How strong has her love become for her God. Beloved, keep your vows of devotion to Jesus and display His love to the world.

When I look at you,
I see how you have taken my fruit and tasted my word.
Your life has become clean and pure,
like a lamb washed and newly shorn.
You now show grace and balance with truth on display. (4:2)

"When I look at you I see how you have taken my fruit and tasted My Word." By tasting the Word, the Shulamite had to taste of it with her teeth. Teeth indicate the Shulamite's ability to eat the strong meat given to her from the Word of God. She has matured enough to chew the solid truths of the Word of God (Heb. 5:13–14). Infants have no teeth to chew their food (1 Cor. 3:1–3); they are not yet able to acquire God's teachings as revelation. We have an abundance of food to eat in the Bible, but few of us have the ability to digest it and make it our own. The bride now has the capacity to take in the deeper truths of God (John 5:39–40).

"Like a lamb washed and newly shorn," God designates sheep as clean animals in the Old Testament. To shear the sheep is to take off the excess wool of fleshly zeal. The removal of the excess wool speaks to us of the energy of the flesh that must be left behind when we move into the Holy Place with God (Ezek. 44:17). There is to be no sweat in God's presence. Priests were instructed not to wear wool so they didn't sweat as they served the Lord. The flesh doesn't need to work harder to please God; rather, it needs to be shorn.

Have you been shorn lately? Jesus sees His bride as one who has been delivered from sweating it out in striving to serve Him. Many of us need to be shorn of the wisdom of the world and renewed in our minds. Striving in the flesh will bring a curse of barrenness (Jer. 17:5–6). The maiden's devotion (hair) is like a lamb just shorn. She has digested the Word and knows that spiritual growth is not by her power and zeal alone, but by the reality of the Scriptures lived out daily.

"Washed." The washing of the Word has cleansed her heart (Eph. 5:25–26; James 1:21). Cleansed from impure and fleshly motives, she has taken the Word and made it her own. As we receive the Word and meditate upon it, our minds are washed and renewed. The Shulamite maiden's mind has been transformed, sanctified, and cleansed by receiving the words of God.

"You now show grace and balance with truth on display," could also be translated as "each has its twin." These "twins" (grace and balance) speak of the balance of wisdom needed in our day-to-day lives. The Shulamite holds on to old truths as she reaches for the new. Balanced and beautiful, she is capable of handling truth in its many-sided features. The bearing of twins also speaks of fruitfulness—the double blessing!

> **Your lips are as lovely as Rahab's scarlet ribbon,**
> **speaking mercy, speaking grace,**
> **the words of your mouth are as refreshing as an oasis.**
> **What pleasure you bring to me!**
> **I see your blushing cheeks**
> **opened like the halves of a pomegranate,**
> **showing through your veil of tender meekness. (4:3)**

"Your lips are as lovely as Rahab's scarlet ribbon." The lips are what are used when we communicate to someone else. The communication of the Shulamite maiden's mouth reveals what is deep in her heart. Her speech has taken on the "scarlet" qualities of redemption as she uses words to bless, not wound, others. She is even able to gently respond to those who oppose her (2 Tim. 2:24–26; Prov. 15:1). Her words have now become lovely, no longer speaking vain or foolish things. Her lips are like a scarlet cord.*

"Speaking mercy, speaking grace." The maiden is now using her speech to redeem and rescue the immature and perishing. Edifying speech releases grace to others (Col. 4:6). As we grow in the virtues of Christ, our words will become like *"apples of gold in settings of silver"* (Prov. 25:11, NASB). This means that we treat others and speak of them with redeeming mercy. When our lips are purged, then we are mature and ready to be a "sent one" for the Lord to use for His glory and purposes (Isa. 6:1–6; James 2:3).

The theme of mercy must be heard from our lips to the

---

* The scarlet cord that Rahab placed outside her wall was a picture of the blood of Christ and His redeeming love (Josh. 2).

despised and bruised of the world. Do your words release grace to others or do they scorch and sear the heart? Have your words been washed in the scarlet flow of redemption? Just as the scarlet thread of Rahab brought redemption to her house when the Israelites overtook Jericho, so the lips of the bride will bring redemption and deliverance to the hurting. May we have lips that always find redeeming qualities in others—even in those who speak evil of us.

"The words of your mouth are as refreshing as an oasis. What pleasure you bring to me!" In the beginning, the maiden had asked for the kisses of His mouth, but now He says of His maturing bride, *"What pleasure you bring to me!"* She has the capacity to share intimacy with her Beloved. Her lips refer to her speech, but the mouth is related to the sweet kisses of worship and adoration that she brings to Him. He finds intimacy with her as He shares His secrets—it is lovely in His sight. Jesus is delighted with the communion they now share.

"I see your blushing cheeks opened like the halves of a pomegranate." The temples or "cheeks" speak of the bride's emotions. From her countenance, she displays the emotions of her heart.* As Jesus looks behind her veil, He sees that the emotions of her heart are toward Him. Her rosy cheeks are like the sweet red fruit of a pomegranate. The Lord finds pleasure in her as her heart has opened up to Him. She is sensitive to shameful things (red from blushing).

All of these emotions are *"showing through your veil of tender meekness."* Her modesty and hidden life before God makes her attractive to the Bridegroom. She is displaying great tenderness to Him without boasting before others. Carved on the very top of the pillars in Solomon's temple were rows of pomegranates (1 Kings 7:20; Rev. 3:12). As the Lord looked down from on high to see His temple, He saw pomegranates opened up before Him. May our lives

---

* Sadness, joy, anger, frustration, etc., are all emotions that are seen on the countenance. Godly emotions can be greatly used by God.

be laid open moment by moment to the gaze of Jesus Christ. "Lord, make our opened hearts a constant delight to You."

It's time to be passionate about the Lord! We can be passionate about so many other things in life, but the most important person we could ever waste our passion on is Jesus. He deserves it all and should be preeminent in all of our lives, lifted high above all other pursuits. Why not determine to be more passionate about Him than all else?

> **When I look at you,**
> **I see your inner strength so stately and strong.**
> **You are as secure as David's fortress.**
> **Your virtues and grace cause a thousand famous soldiers**
> **to surrender to your beauty. (4:4)**

"You (or your neck) *are as secure as David's fortress."* The neck represents the will of a person. Those stubborn and proud of heart are called "stiff-necked," while those with a yielded will often bow their necks (heads) in humility and submission. And the Shulamite has submitted her will completely to her King, causing her to be stately and strong. She is strong, resolute, and secure in all that He is. Just as He is, so she is in this world.

Conquering kings would put their feet upon the necks of their enemies to show that they had prevailed over them, but she will surrender to no other king but King Jesus! The maiden's will, yielded to the King, is a beautiful feature of the maturing bride of Christ. Her neck (compared to a fortress) speaks of her security and strength in doing the right thing, no matter the cost. She is no longer double-minded. He tells her, "You are standing on solid spiritual ground with a resolute will to fulfill My destiny for you. I can see you will not be turned aside to lesser pursuits." Her will is now like the heart of David (Ps. 57:7).

Like David, the Shulamite has resolutely fixed her will to go after her Beloved. David's tower was a place where the weapons of warfare were stored.* The Shulamite's voluntary decision to follow the King is like a storehouse of mighty weapons against the opposition of Satan. He views her inward life and resolute will as an armory full of offensive weapons. Nehemiah referred to an armory near the king's tower (Neh. 3:19, 25).

**Your pure faith and love rest over your heart
as you nurture those who are yet infants. (4:5)**

Like a nursing mother, the church will give sustenance to her young. But what kind of life substance will she impart? Faith and love, for *"faith and love rest over your heart..."* She is releasing the right kind of life to those who are led to the Savior. Like twin fawns of a gazelle that have fed on lilies (purity of heart), she is able to multiply a double-portion to those she has touched. Her sacred affections are pure and imparted to the young and immature. She has fed herself properly among those pure of heart and is quite able to nurture others.

Paul said that we are to put on *"faith and love as a breastplate"* (1 Thess. 5:8), which are the two qualities seen in her life as the maturing bride. When faith and love are combined, they form righteousness before God and men. These enduring traits of Christlikeness are now developed and affirmed from Jesus to His church. Not only is she growing in maturity, but she is able to nourish and impart life to others.

Pray this prayer today: "Lord Jesus, I can see now that Your grace is transforming my life. The more I understand and embrace Your love, the more I am changed. I love the way You bring me into spiritual maturity. Your love casts out my fear and brings me closer to You. I am grateful for all You are doing in my life. I love You, Lord Jesus! Amen."

---

* Solomon, David's son, would know very well about his father's armory.

CHAPTER 19

I WILL
GO WITH YOU

I've made up my mind.
Until the darkness disappears and the dawn has fully come,
in spite of shadows and fears,
I will go to the mountaintop with you—
the mountain of suffering love and the hill of burning incense.
Yes, I will be your bride. (4:6)

After hearing these eight prophetic affirmations over her life, the Shulamite maiden is now willing to leave her comfort zone behind. She is ready to leave the predictable place from behind her wall and go to the mountaintops with her beloved King. She has learned much thus far; now her heart is prepared for the high places of warfare and intercession. The bride is ready to be trained and discipled for the King.

At this point in the song, the maiden from Shunem makes a life-changing decision. From this point forward, she will never be the same again. His love has conquered her. His eyes of passion for her have melted away the fear of the high places. She arises with fresh determination to pay the price and go to the mountain of myrrh. The combination of His discipline (3:1–5), the new revelation of how safe He really is (3:6–11), and His undying love expressed to her has completely melted her heart. Now she is ready for the mountains. Every fear in her heart has been removed—she will arise and go.

I will go to the mountaintop with you—
the mountain of suffering love. (4:6)

This was the challenge to which she said no earlier. Jesus is so wise and capable of changing our hearts, no matter how fickle and stubborn and fearful they may be. So often we resist the challenges of spiritual growth, only later to say yes and take His hand. Real change in our life does not come by gritting our teeth and trying harder, but by falling in love with our King more and more each day. His affection for us breaks the power of a thousand sins. He is preparing you and me for the high place and for greater degrees of spiritual warfare.

But what really are we saying yes to? Do we even know what it means to go with Him to the mountaintop? To go to the *"mountain of suffering"* is to embrace the cross, the death of selfishness within. He stands as one who leaps over the mountains, saying, "Arise and come!"

It is time to embrace the cross unto self-denying love, as we pour out our lives for the nations. To say yes to the mountain of myrrh is a lifetime commitment to embrace the cross. There is a life principle that the end-time bride will understand here—it is the reality of the cross. More than an event, or an emblem, it is the tree of life, Jacob's ladder, and the burning bush. To the mountain of myrrh every seeking heart will go, and it is there that we find Him. This is where we are taught the ways of God and where we discover self-abandonment. We must learn the same lesson that the maiden learned. The days when we only sought our own pleasure are over when we choose to be a faithful bride.

The *"hill of burning incense"* is the place of abandoned intercession and worship. A hill is smaller than a mountain, so it is the hill of incense that enables us to scale the mountain of myrrh. Every passionate believer must learn the lessons of self-abandoned worship and intercession. None of us are sufficient to scale mountains and run with Jesus without a deepening life of prayer. Our incense is our prayer to God before His throne (Rev. 5:8; Ps. 141:2). This is true communion with God in the heavenlies while we embrace a life of self-denial on earth. Through our ascended life, we climb the hill of incense, finding resurrection power in our prayers.

"Until the darkness disappears and the dawn has fully come, in spite of shadows and fears…" The day is the time of total victory over darkness. The Shulamite makes the inner vow that she will go with Jesus to the place of the cross until all her dark shadows have fled, until the light of His day has removed all of her imperfections. The Shulamite maiden will live with Him on the hill of incense and the mountain of myrrh until all her compromises have been dealt with in His glorious presence. She will continue on the mountain of myrrh while cultivating a life of intercession on the hill of frankincense. This is where the bride begins to emerge without spot and wrinkle. The greater anointing found on *"the mountain of suffering love"* will accomplish this until she finally says, *"Yes, I will be your bride."*

Every part of you is so beautiful, my darling.
Perfect your beauty without flaw within. (4:7)

What will His response be to all of this? Her decision to run with Him brought forth a fresh affirmation: *"Every part of you is so beautiful, my darling…without flaw within."* Can you imagine hearing Jesus say this to you today? You are altogether ravishing to His heart! He speaks again of her inward beauty coming forth. She is His darling, His lover-friend. Not "you will be" but "you are" right now…even before you ascend the hill of the Lord. All He sees in her is the beauty of her abandonment to Him. She is not merely beautiful, but *"so beautiful."*

Her whole life is summed up in these words, *"without flaw*

within." This doesn't mean she is without sin, for she has not yet passed the ultimate test she is to endure in chapter 5. Yet her willingness to embrace the cross and run with Him has delighted His heart. Jesus sees in her an undying desire to take all that He will teach her and walk in the light she has found in Him. Perfect love has begun to cast out her fear. The apostle Paul speaks of a bride without spot or blemish, prepared for the heavenly Bridegroom. This bride is now making herself ready each time she yields to the higher calling of being one with Christ on the mountaintop.

If He had said there is no hideous scar, no horrible deformity, no deadly ulcer, we might even then have marveled; but when He testifies that she is free from the slightest spot, all these other forms of defilement are included, and the depths of wonder are increased. If He had but promised to remove all spots by-and-by, we should have had eternal reason for joy; but when He speaks of it as already done, who can restrain the most intense emotions of satisfaction and delight?

"Come with me." The King invites her to come into intimate partnership with Him, to look at the nations from His point of view. She is now being discipled in the heavenly perspective of what God wants to do among the people of the earth. In the high place, she can see what had confused her in the past. This is an invitation for her to be taught lessons of higher levels of spiritual warfare and be equipped to sit as a bride at His side. Lebanon's peaks, where the lions and leopards roam, are the places of advanced spiritual warfare. Now she ascends with Him to engage in active service and partnership with Jesus.*

Now you are ready, bride of the mountains,
to come with me as we climb the highest peaks together.
Come with me through the archway of trust.
We will look down from the crest of the glistening mounts

---

* This is really where He wanted to take her in 2:10–13.

and from the summit of our sublime sanctuary.
Together we will wage war in the lion's den and the leopard's lair
as they watch nightly for their prey. (4:8)

Now He calls her *"bride."* This is the first reference to her as the bride of Christ in the song. *"Now you are ready, bride of the mountains, to come with me as we climb the highest peaks together."* She has come forth from her darkness to skip with Him on the mountains. This shows that she truly has bridal affection for the Son of God. Her passion for Him has taken her to the cross and a life of intercession. As His beautiful bride, they take a journey together to the high place and view the world from His perspective as eternal partners. In the final hours of the church age, it will be the Spirit and the bride who says, "Come!" This bridal cry will intensify until our passion is to know Him as our husband (Hos. 2:16).

To be called His bride means that all the privileges of the relationship become ours. To be called His spouse, His cherished one, even when we can still remember all the times we fought Him and His perfect will for our lives, is utterly astounding. We are heirs of all things when we become His bride. Everything He has is now ours. Our poverty is drowned out in the riches of His redeeming love.

Although a picture of spiritual warfare, Lebanon's mountains were also known for their breathtaking beauty (Lebanon means "snowy mountain"). The glory of Lebanon is mentioned in Isaiah 35:2. Jesus's countenance is like Lebanon (5:15; Hos. 14:6), Moses longed to see Lebanon (Deut. 3:25), and Solomon built a summer home in Lebanon because of its forests. This view from the high place is symbolic of where we have already been seated with Christ in the heavenly places (Eph. 2:6; Col. 3:1–4). She must now focus on the eternal, what is unseen, rather than merely the natural world (2 Cor. 4:8; 5:7). It is time for the bride to look from the top of the mountain.

"From the crest* of the glistening mounts and from the summit of our sublime sanctuary." These are the realms of the Spirit where true realities are understood. These are the highest peaks that give view to the land of promise. Many of the saints have stood on these high peaks to look into the realm of God and see what He was about to release to the earth. The end-time church will be given startling revelations that have been undisclosed until now (Dan. 12). Israel had to conquer Amorite kings before they could scale this mountain range, so the flesh life of each of us must be subdued and broken before true revelation comes.

"Together we will wage war in the lion's den and the leopard's lair as they watch nightly for their prey." Lions and leopards are the spiritual forces of evil that roam in the high places (Eph. 6:12). Satan is called a roaring lion, seeking to devour people through fear (1 Peter 5:7–8). Now the maiden is taking her place at the King's side as He wars against demonic principalities in the Devil's hideout (Hab. 2:17; Ps. 57:4). To face him with holy power we must daily embrace the cross, even when forgotten by others.

The story began with a cry for a kiss, now we find the bride being prepared as a warrior. The Hebrew word for *kiss* is *nashaq*, a homonym that can also mean "to arm for battle," and "to be equipped for war." Perhaps it is the kiss that equips us for battle. Every warrior must begin with being a lover, and every lover will end up being a warrior.

Pray this prayer today: "Help me, Lord Jesus, to love You with a love that will never quit or shrink back. I want my love for You to prepare me for the battles I face. Even under pressure, I love You. Even when life is difficult, I pledge my love to You, King of Glory. Amen."

---

* The crest of Amana, which is the seal of covenant. *Amana* comes from a Hebrew root word from which we get the English word *amen*. This is also one of the Hebrew words for "faith." The crest of Amana is the realm where all God's promises are kept and realized. Amana can also be translated "a place of settled security" (*Dictionary of Scripture Proper Names*, J. B. Jackson).

CHAPTER 20

THE RAVISHED HEART OF JESUS

For you reach into my heart.
With one flash of your eyes I am undone by your love,
my beloved, my equal, my bride.
You leave me breathless—
I am overcome by merely a glance from your worshipping eyes,
for you have stolen my heart.
I am held hostage by your love
and by the graces of righteousness shining upon you. (4:9)

J esus, the King of all the ages, unveils His heart of love to the maiden. For all eternity He has longed for a bride, a partner to sit with Him on His throne. Now He tells her just what He thinks of her. Beloved, *you* are the one He speaks to like this. Can't you hear Him telling you that you have conquered His heart?

Her love has simply ravished His heart. She has said yes to the mountains of myrrh, she is willing to embrace the cross. It's as though He can see the fear in her eyes, so the King reassures her in love: "You will be safe, dear one. Every time you glance at Me, My heart skips a beat." Have you ever wondered how Jesus really feels about you? This verse gives us an answer few are prepared to handle.

Jesus wants to reveal His passion and enjoyment of *you—yes, you!* He wants to describe how you have thrilled His heart. The Creator of emotions wants to show His emotions toward you. Get ready to receive the most astonishing love from the very heart and lips of Jesus Christ. Your worship makes His heart beat faster.

Imagine for a moment that the heart of God is ravished over you right now—not just later when you live better. In the mess of life, Jesus is completely overjoyed with you. This phrase *"you have stolen my heart"* can be translated as "you have made my heart skip a beat." He is saying to us today, "You have enchanted and enthralled My heart! You have brought ecstasy to My heart! You have made My heart swell with joy." Need He say more?

Jesus's heart is filled with an extravagant, furious love that can never be quenched. His loving affection for His people can barely be described. He is overcome with emotions of joy and delight every time you come to His mind (which is all the time). His heart is captivated with love for human beings even while they are insecure, weak, and imperfect. This is the love of Jesus that will demolish strongholds of rejection and the negative thoughts that are entrenched in human hearts. Nothing is more powerful than omnipotent love. His passion for you is all consuming and relentless.

The same way the Father loves the Son is the way Jesus loves you: *"I love each of you with the same love that the Father loves me. Let my love nourish your hearts"* (John 15:9). Sooner or later it will dawn on you: God could not love you any more than He does right now. If you are better tomorrow, He will not love you more; if you are worse tomorrow, He will not love you any less. The tractor beam of divine love has fully and completely captured you.

Our hearts must be able to rest in the undisturbed love of Jesus, or the shaking around us will affect the sweet communion of our hearts with Him. It is not enough that we understand what He did on the cross or what He will do in the coming revival—we must know about His deepest desires for us and how He feels about us.

This gives us insight into His personality and why He does what He does. Discipled in love, we will not be moved or shaken.

Others are not as kind as Jesus. Only the Son of God can see loveliness in us when others see our grime. Jesus wears grace glasses. As God sees us growing and fulfilling our purpose in life, joy floods His heart. Our glance of love is what He died for. So we must keep looking at Jesus until we hear Him say, *"I am overcome by merely a glance from your worshipping eyes, for you have stolen my heart."*

Jesus cannot resist one look from the eyes of one who is sincere in seeking Him. Lift up your eyes to Him today. Why are you so downcast? One glance from your eyes and you will have ravished the heart of the Son of God. It is not the gifted ones who have stolen His heart; it is the yielded ones. We do not really understand what our worship does to the heart of Jesus Christ. Beloved, hear this prophetic word over you:

> Let Me tell you what you mean to Me, My beloved bride. Every time you look at Me in worship and adoration, you capture My heart. You enflame My heart when you look to Me out of your place of pain and isolation. I am energized once again to perfect your love and change you into My image. One glance from your eyes does to Me what the armies and kings could not do—you have conquered Me fully. I will give you all that I have to make you My partner, My bride. I am for you. You are willing to learn the lessons of the dark trails on the mountain of myrrh. I turn to you even as you turn to Me. Your thoughts of Me, your prayers to Me in the night seasons, your love and obedience to Me have become delightful—more than wine! Pursue Me even if you don't sense that I am near. Come, seek Me. I will be found by you, My bride!

How satisfying to me, my equal, my bride.
Your love is my finest wine—intoxicating and thrilling.
And your sweet, perfumed praises—so exotic, so pleasing. (4:10)

In most translations 4:10 reads, *"How satisfying you are to me my sister, my bride."* I don't know about you, but where I come from sister and bride should not be in the same sentence! Where I come from a sister-bride is illegal. But when I researched the meaning in the original languages, I found that sister could actually be speaking of a being of like nature, one from the same family (Heb. 2:10–18; Matt. 12:49–50). How incredible and humbling that Jesus would take our nature upon Himself and by the resurrection give us His. He is not ashamed to call us brother or sister. He calls us part of His family, claiming for Himself a relationship with us in the family of grace. But what is even more incredible than that is that *sister* could actually be translated *equal.* He calls us His *"equal."* Can you fathom that? His equal!

Doesn't it say in Scripture that we are not to be unequally yoked? So do you think the Father would yoke His Son with someone who is not His equal? This fact is going to take us a long time to understand, but we do know, as it says in 1 John, that when we see Him, we shall be like Him, His coequal. Did you know you're co-crucified and co-raised with Him in His resurrection power? We are coheirs at the side of Jesus for all eternity. Jesus loves His bride. You are His nearest and dearest.

"Your love is my finest wine—intoxicating and thrilling." These are the words the Shulamite maiden used in speaking to Him. Now He turns to her and says it back to her: *"Your love is my finest wine!"* He is essentially saying, "You are more pleasing to Me than anything else in the created universe." It's true. My cold, feeble love is precious to the Lord Jesus. He calls my love for Him *"his finest wine—intoxicating and thrilling."* Jesus values our love more than any other pleasure there is. He measures it not by its strength, but by its sincerity. He knows we love Him although we fail and sin at times.

You are His banqueting table. Your heart is a love feast for Jesus. When you long for Him and are drawn by bridal affection into the waves of worship, then you are delightful to the Son of God. Beautiful and pleasing are your ways when you pour out pure worship to Him. He desires love more than your sacrificial works of ministry (Hos. 6:7; 1 Cor. 13:3; Rev. 2:1–5).

The love of all the angels combined cannot be compared to your love poured out to Him. All the joys of paradise are nothing to the joys He experiences in spending time with you. Have you ever wondered how Jesus feels about your prayers? I bet you think your prayer life stinks, right? But Jesus says it smells like perfume—*"and your sweet, perfumed praises—so exotic, so pleasing."* Our intercession and worship is a fragrant perfume to the King.

Jesus is saying to you, "Your love is My finest wine. Your virtues are My sweet praise-perfume." She has spent so much time with Him that her praises now have His scent upon them. His fragrance is upon her. How incredible to think that we are able to minister to Him, to delight His heart in such a way as this.

Paul mentions the fragrance as the sweet aroma of Christ that comes forth from the redeemed (2 Cor. 2:14–16). This was written to one of the most messed up churches in the New Testament—the church at Corinth. To God, our devotional life is more pleasing than any spice, regardless of what we think is lacking.

Rare and exquisite spices were exchanged as gifts among royalty. The Queen of Sheba gave spices as a gift to Solomon (1 Kings 10:2), wise men brought spices to Jesus at His birth because they knew He was a King (Matt. 2:11), and these same spices were also included in the sacred anointing oil that God instructed Moses to make (Exod. 30:23–24). Our love for Jesus, our prayers to Him, our weak worship, our thoughts toward Him—they all blend to form the finest fragrance of sacred devotion to the Lord, *"so exotic, so pleasing."*

> **Your loving words are like the honeycomb to me;**
> **your tongue releases milk and honey,**
> **for I find the Promised Land flowing within you.**
> **The fragrance of your worshipping love**
> **surrounds you with scented robes of white. (4:11)**

Your King notices your every word, and He hears the sigh of your heart as you lean toward Him: "Your loving words are like the honeycomb to me." The lips, of course, refer to our speech (see notes on 4:3). The words that the bride speaks to God and to others are like sweet honey. Jesus notices every word that comes from the lips of His bride: "Nothing is more appealing than speaking beautiful, life-giving words. For they release sweetness to our souls and inner healing to our spirits" (Prov. 16:24).

"Your tongue releases milk and honey, for I find the Promised Land flowing within you." The bride has filled herself with milk and honey, which are both emblems of the Word of God (Isa. 7:15). When she speaks, the honey of spiritual revelation and milk of nourishing truths are under her tongue. These are the two foods given to babes. The bride is now nourishing others with loving words that spring from her mouth.

Milk and honey also characterized the abundance of the Promised Land. There is an abundance of kindness and wisdom in all that she spoke. *"Under your tongue"* means that her heart and her words are in agreement with one another. Her private thoughts are pondered in her heart before she speaks them; she holds them under her tongue with honey and cream. The lips and tongue are the channel of her ministry; her speech has changed.

"Your worshipping love surrounds you with robes of white." Her robes refer to acts of service that she performs out of loving worship for the King (Rev. 19:6–8). Every deed of humble service, regardless of how insignificant it may seem to you, will not go unnoticed by the King of all Kings (Heb. 6:10). Jesus views her everyday ministry as fragrant, carrying the aroma of His life.

Paul spoke of the offerings to his ministry from the church at Philippi as a fragrant aroma of the sacrifice of Christ, which was pleasing to God (Phil. 4:18). Jesus sees your devoted deeds and calls them good and pure. The garments of royal ministry are upon you. You smell good to Jesus. The garlic smell of Egypt has been replaced by the fragrance of the forest in Lebanon. When you put on Christ as your robe of righteousness and purity, His life covers you in His glorious aroma.

Pray this prayer today: "Lord Jesus, I am so thankful to know You and that You have come to me and call me forward. I want to run with You wherever You may take me. I want to be Your loving partner. I want to enter into Your prayer life and Your passion for others. Bring me into that realm of sharing Your glory and knowing You as You really are. I love You, Lord Jesus. Amen."

CHAPTER 21

HIS PRIVATE PARADISE

My darling bride, my private paradise, fastened to my heart.
A secret spring are you that no one else can have—
my bubbling fountain hidden from public view.
What a perfect partner to me now that I have you. (4:12)

The heart of the bride is the private paradise of King Jesus. An enclosed garden would be used only for the King—a place for His pleasure, for His enjoyment. Once the Shulamite maiden was a wilderness overgrown with weeds, but now she is His fruitful garden: *"A secret spring are you that no one else can have—my bubbling fountain hidden from public view."*

It is said that King Solomon had an enclosed garden that he would often retreat to for solitude and rest. Beloved, you are *"a secret spring"* and *"a bubbling fountain"* in that garden that has only one use—to bring pleasure to your Creator. This secret spring and bubbling fountain are not found in a garden used for agriculture, but a place of fellowship and communion with the living God. God placed man and woman in a garden as a picture of what our relationship with Him was to be like, a place where He finds refreshment and enjoyment from drinking from the secret spring, bubbling up like a fountain from the rivers of life flowing from within you (1 Cor. 3:6–9).

Our hearts must be His enclosed Eden, with a gate locked to the world, reserved only for the King. Our inner castle, where we dwell in His chambers, must be kept locked for His use only. Our imaginations and fantasies must flow from our love for our beautiful Lord Jesus. The enemy will come to ruin that serene place and try to muddy the waters, but he must be kept out of the locked gate, where only purity can enter.

God told Cain that *"sin is crouching at the door"* (Gen. 4:7, NASB), and Jesus told His church, *"Behold I stand at the door and knock"* (Rev. 3:20, NASB). Both sin and Jesus want to enter our hearts. When we see ourselves as His *"spring"* that *"no one else can have,"* only our Lord Jesus will be able enter. Out of this *"secret spring"* and *"bubbling fountain"* relationship will flow true life and ministry bearing fruit for His glory. The bride's life passions are locked up and sealed. The Bridegroom's very glory is all around her. Jesus's bride is not open to sin but is protected from the Devil, enjoyed exclusively by Jesus. God will help us live in this truth if we really seek it with a whole heart.

There is a place in God where temptation will not overcome you (1 Cor. 10:13). Jesus really can keep us from falling (Jude 24). Our inner wilderness can become His Eden, His garden of delight, with secret springs and bubbling fountains. No one can plunder His locked garden, for He alone holds the key. The fresh water spring found within waters the King's garden, a private spring that is not polluted by any outside source. It is a covered spring that cannot be defiled by unclean things. The Shulamite is not a watering hole for wild animals that would muddy the spring, but a drinking fountain for her Beloved. For the bride refuses to be polluted by the things of this world; she is reserved for only the King. Her clean life brings refreshing to His heart. Out of her inner being flows this living water. *"The Lord will guide you always; he will satisfy your needs in a sun-scorched land and will strengthen your frame. You will be a well-watered garden, like a spring whose waters never fail"* (Isa. 58:11, NIV).

It is *secret*. Our secret thoughts and meditations are like cool streams of water to our King. Our inner life is a secret spring that is open only to Jesus, who alone knows the way to enter our heart. There is a mysterious life within that no human can touch. It is a secret that no other person knows. It's separated, uncommon, and private. It's not the common spring, of which every passer-by may drink; it is one kept and preserved from all others. It's a fountain bearing a particular mark—a king's royal seal—so that all can perceive that it is not a common fountain, but a fountain owned by a proprietor and placed specially by itself alone.

So is it with the spiritual life. The chosen of God were separated in the eternal decree; God separated them in the day of redemption; and they are separated by the possession of a life that others don't have. It is impossible for them to feel at home with the world, or to delight in its pleasures. And Jesus Himself drinks from this cistern (Prov. 5:15).

There is a legend that King Solomon had a secret sealed fountain known only to him. He had it sealed in such a way that only with his signet ring could it be opened and the water able to flow. The doors of the secret spring would open up, releasing sweet waters of which no one could drink except him. We have become Jesus's holy and sacred fountain, sealed by the Holy Spirit (Eph. 4:30). Every Christian should feel that he or she has God's seal upon them. We should be able to say with Paul, *"From henceforth let no man trouble me, for I bear in my body the marks of the Lord Jesus"* (Gal. 6:17, NASB).

It is *secure*! How sure and safe is the inner life of the believer! If all the powers of earth and hell were to unite against it, it is still kept safe by the blood of the Lamb and by the one who gave His life for its preservation. For who is he who shall harm you when God is your protector?

The Bridegroom knows the pathway into your spirit, and with His touch (kiss) the fountains flow. Jesus knows what melody moves you. Your heart melts when He sings His song over you.

Your inward life is now sprouting, bringing forth fruit.
What a beautiful paradise unfolds within you.
When I'm near you, I smell aromas of the finest spice,
for many clusters of my exquisite fruit
now grow within your inner garden.
Here are the nine:
pomegranates of passion,
henna from heaven,
spikenard so sweet,
saffron shining,
fragrant calamus from the cross,
sacred cinnamon,
branches of scented woods,
myrrh, like tears from a tree,
and aloe as eagles ascending. (4:13–14)

"I find many clusters of my exquisite fruit now grow within your inner garden." The church is like a garden, full of pleasant fruits, with diverse plants and spices. We are not a barren wilderness. Jesus gazes at His bride and views us as the most pleasant fruitful garden filled with many trees and plants. We are each one a delight to Him with our different gifts and expressions of worship. Here are nine of them.

"Pomegranates of passion." The pomegranate is a sweet fruit that must be broken open before it can be eaten. When we are broken open to God, our ministry becomes sweet to Him and to others. The pomegranate is a symbol of pure and golden thoughts with passion for the Bridegroom, opening up for Him. This choice fruit is a delight to others as she impacts the nations with the fruits of passion and desire, yielding a life of fruitfulness for Him (Isa. 51:3).

She is now filled with the fragrance of His love, His joy, and His peace (Gal. 5:22–23). The nine fruits of the Spirit are coming out of her personality as the King shines forth. Rare and exquisite spices are being brought out as the beauty of her devoted heart is revealed. She has become a fruit-filled garden full of delight and pleasure for the King. By dwelling on the Word, she is constantly filled with His life.

These exotic fruits and spices have to be imported because they come from another land. The heavenly life of the Spirit is now blooming within as symbolized by these nine spices and flowers.

"Henna from heaven." Henna comes from a tree whose leaves yield a fluid used as red dye. The primary root word for *henna* means "to forgive." It signifies the shed blood of the cross, the costly work of God that has brought the bride into the fragrance of Christ. The maiden had used henna blossoms to describe the Lord earlier (1:14), but now He uses the same term to describe her inward life. He recognizes His likeness sprouting forth in her.

In the ancient Jewish tradition, the night before the wedding, the bride's hands and feet were stained with henna. The bride of the crucified Lamb is to exude the sweet smell of forgiveness in her works (hands) and her walk (feet). We are to be those who continually release forgiveness and mercy to others.

"Spikenard so sweet." Spikenard is the fragrance that Mary poured on the feet of Jesus (John 12:3). Pure nard is an extremely costly spice, taken from the dried stems of a plant that grows high in the Himalayas, where the sun is strong and pure. The Hebrew root of *nard* is "light." Jesus Christ is the true light, for in Him there is no darkness at all (1 John 1:5). The bride must live as one with Him in perfect light—nothing hidden and nothing in the shadows. We are to be those lampstands in His Holy Place.

Eventually, even our shadows will be so infused with light from God that the sick will be healed when we walk by them, as it was with Peter in the book of Acts (Acts 5:15). The maiden first smelled this spikenard as she sat at the King's table of abundance (1:12). Our worship is the sweetest perfume to the nostrils of our King.

"Saffron shining" is the crocus, the Lover's perfume, which is both costly and fragrant. The Shulamite adores the Son of God. Saffron can also mean yellowish orange, referring to the gold of His character shining on her walk. Saffron is a costly and valuable spice that is worth its weight in gold.

Faith is also valuable. Peter reminds us all that our *"faith, being more precious than gold which is perishable, even though tested by fire, may be found to result in praise and glory and honor at the revelation of Jesus Christ"* (1 Peter 1:7, NASB). The faith of Jesus was proved genuine in every testing He endured, and this golden faith has now been given to you as the sweetest spice in your heart.

"Fragrant calamus from the cross." Calamus is taken from a marsh plant known as "sweet flag" that produces fragrant oil. The Hebrew word for this spice means "erect or upright." God's poetic name for Israel was "Jeshurun," which means "upright one" (Isa. 44:2). And we know that Jesus is the true upright one. As His chosen ones, we are to walk in righteousness and be upright in His grace (Isa. 26:7).

"Cinnamon" emits a fragrance that is representative of an odor of holiness to the Lord. This was used in the sacred anointing oil of the priests and the tabernacle. It was one of the holy ingredients used to set apart those called to divine service. Our consecration to Christ is to be like cinnamon to Him and to the world.

"Branches of scented woods" speaks of the fragrant cedars or trees of frankincense. They represent the purity of devotion of the resurrected Christ as He intercedes before the Father. His prayers rise like incense to the throne of grace. Our Lord Jesus is set apart to this wonderful ministry of intercession night and day. As our magnificent intercessor, He releases the Spirit of grace and supplication in our lives.

The soothing aroma of a life filled with God is now being released from the bride. Every variety of frankincense is pouring forth from her. These trees had to be cut to give forth their fragrance, just as the bride must be broken before the fragrance of Jesus spills forth.

"Myrrh, like tears from a tree," is the suffering fragrance that constantly reminds the maiden of the costly sacrifice of Jesus on the cross. The spice of myrrh comes from the pierced bark of a thorny tree. What a clear picture of the cross and sufferings of our Lord Jesus. He was a Son who learned obedience from the things that He suffered (Heb. 5:8).

Jesus emptied Himself of His own will and joyfully came to earth, knowing what was awaiting Him. Each believer is likewise called to exude this fragrance of a heart walking in full obedience to Christ by denying our own self-life. When we walk through every valley with Jesus, we are entering into *"the fellowship of His sufferings"* (Phil. 3:10).

"Aloe as the eagles ascending" is considered by many as a healing balm. The presence of the Lord within her is now released as healing balm to those she touches. The psalmist tells us that Jesus's robes smelled of aloes (Ps. 45:8). One of the names used by some for aloes is the word *eagle*. Like eagles, we fly above our wounds, free from the past as we walk in intimacy with Him. Loving the Bridegroom heals the heart (Rom. 8:28).

The young bride is full of fruit and fragrance. Her life is delightful and pleasing to her Beloved. Her sweet pomegranates and pleasant fruits speak of having a pleasant impact on others. Fragrant henna with spikenard speaks of the precious and costly work of the Spirit in our life. Spikenard and saffron, calamus and cinnamon speak of the various graces seen in her ministry. Her trees of frankincense speak of a ministry of prayer. Myrrh and aloes remind us of the cross and death to self. With all the finest spices, the bride's life now speaks of grace imparted to others through her ministry (2 Cor. 2:14–16). What an amazing transformation has taken place before His very eyes.

Your life flows into mine, pure as a garden spring.
A well of living water springs up from within you,
like a mountain brook flowing into my heart! (4:15)

"Like a mountain brook" she flows into the Bridegroom's heart. She is His garden of Eden, His sanctuary. His love has built a wall around her—no one else can have her. *"Your life flows into mine, pure as a garden spring...you [are] like a mountain brook."* The literal Hebrew reads, *"You are a fountain of gardens, a well of living water."* She is His sanctuary from which the river of life is flowing (Ezek. 47:12). Jesus prophesied that "streams of living water will flow from within" (John 7:37–38). She has an inward source of supply and grace. As His garden spring, she springs up with fresh zeal and affection for Him.

Pray this prayer today: "Lord Jesus, thank You for calling me Your private paradise, Your garden of delight. I give You my heart and hold nothing back from You today. My praise is Yours, my life is Yours, my family is Yours, my finances are Yours, and my health and strength is in Your hands. Thank You for making me one with You. I love You this day, Lord Jesus. Amen."

CHAPTER 22

A CRY FOR MORE

Then may your awakening breath
blow upon my life until I am fully yours.
Breathe upon me with your Spirit wind.
Stir up the sweet spice of your life within me.
Spare nothing as you make me your fruitful garden.
Hold nothing back until I release your fragrance.
Come walk with me as you walked
with Adam in your paradise garden.
Come taste the fruits of your life in me. (4:16–5:1)

The Shulamite has heard these words from the Lord. She knows now that she is His garden of delight, His garden of Eden. The words spoken to the maiden were a declaration of confidence from her Lover prompting her to cry for the *"Spirit wind."* The King knew just what she needed to become more anointed as His vessel of grace.

The fruits and spices of a life yielded to Him are now in full bloom within her. The water of life is flowing from her inner being. She flings her arms wide open and bursts forth with, *"Spare nothing as you make me your fruitful garden. Hold nothing back until I release your fragrance."* This is an incredible cry coming from the depths of her heart. The Shulamite asks for the breath of heaven to stir her garden and unlock the fragrances in her heart. Looking away from herself, she begins to prophesy to the winds to begin to stir her life. The north wind is the cold, biting wind of adversity. Does she really want the north wind to blow upon her heart?

She is willing to embrace difficult circumstances if they will make fruit grow and His fragrance spread in her life. The bride cries for the north wind to be awakened and do its work in her soul. Have you been blown away yet by the breath of the Spirit of God? With an unexpected fierceness, the north wind will one day blow upon every passionate heart that yearns for Him.

There are some issues of God's training in our lives that can only result from testing and trials. Deep pockets of unperceived pride, self-confidence, anger, and fear will only be exposed by the cold and cutting blast of the north winds. The Shulamite now understands the importance of adversity in the process of maturing into a fragrant garden for God. She cries out for more discipline, more training: "Whatever it takes to make me like You, Lord! Awaken Spirit winds. Come do Your work in me. Blow on my garden. Blow on my ministry. Blow on my life in You. Finish the work of bringing forth Your life in me."

It was the north wind that broke Mary's alabaster box and released the fragrance of her garden throughout the house where Jesus was dining that day. Humbling our heart in repentance and brokenness will release His fragrance, but so often we are unwilling to go there. We must ask the Lord to send us *anything* that will release kingdom life in us. The Lord will someday bring us to the place in our relationship with Him where external circumstances are not our delight, but the Lord Himself will be our joy and our strength. This is the heritage of the servants of the Lord. Cry for the north wind, beloved!

What about the south wind? This is the mild breeze of refreshing, the cool breeze of grace that blesses and caresses. It is divine love warming the bride's heart. She asks for the comforter to come. She realizes that it takes both adversity and blessing to bring the aroma of Christ from within her.

Ezekiel prophesied to the winds to blow, and life came into dry bones. When the winds blow, when His breath blows upon her garden, all that is dead within her springs to life. At times, the north wind and south wind will blow all at once in order to swiftly mature us and release divine fragrance from our garden.

The goat-keeping maiden is truly becoming like the one she loves. What matters most to her is that her garden-fragrance is released in her daily life. The wind that blows on her garden is the breath of the Lord bringing grace and equipping mercy. *Wind* and *breath* are the same word in Hebrew. There is a blow and a flow. The Shulamite's desire is to have a life filled with God's power and anointing, filled so completely that others smell Him when they are around her.

For the first time in the Song of Songs, the maiden sees her life and ministry as His garden. The words of love from the Bridegroom's lips have worked powerfully in her. Love has opened her eyes. Revelation is flowing. Understanding is developing. She belongs to Him. All of life is about Him, not just her. The bride longs for the King to come to His garden (her inner life and ministry) and taste the fruits of His grace. She wants Jesus to come and enjoy what the Spirit has done within her. She waits for a visitation from the heavenly Bridegroom.

"Come taste the very fruits of your life in me." She prays, "Come enjoy Yourself in me." Everything in this garden is grown by Him and grown for Him. Since she is His inheritance, she invites Him to enjoy it (Eph. 1:18). Her whole life has changed focus from what *she* gets out of it to what *He* gets out of her. The love song of Jesus is maturing the bride. Can He feast His heart in you? Jesus awaits your invitation.

The Bridegroom-King responds to her:

I have come to you, my darling bride,
for you are my paradise garden! (5:1)

What satisfaction Jesus finds in His church! From this point on He says "My" over and over when referring to her—she has truly become His very own. The ownership of her life and ministry has been transferred over to Him: *my darling bride...my paradise garden.*" Jesus now answers her prayer in 4:16. He has come to His garden to enjoy His inheritance. This is a wonderful time of nearness for her. She has changed, so she asks of Him:

Come walk with me until I am fully yours.
Come taste the fruits of your life in me. (5:1)

The maiden is now able to give her love more fully to Him. The bride understands that her identity is a lover of God. She is moving into advanced stages of dedication. For now, she is the garden of delight to the King. The King now enjoys his inheritance, and so He says:

I have gathered from your heart,
my equal, my bride,
I have gathered from my garden
all my sacred spices—even my myrrh.
I have tasted and enjoyed my wine within you.
I have tasted with pleasure my pure milk, my honeycomb,
which you yield to me.
I delight in gathering my sacred spice,
all the fruits of my life I have
gathered from within you, my paradise garden.
Come, all my friends—
feast upon my bride, all you revelers of my palace.
Feast on her, my lovers!
Drink and drink, and drink again,
until you can take no more.
Drink the wine of her love.
Take all you desire, you priests.
My life within her will become your feast. (5:1)

The Lord comes to His church to gather from us what He has worked within us.* Jesus comes to draw from our hearts the expressions of love and adoration He deserves. He visits us to see if we have embraced His cross (myrrh) and have experienced the graces of God in our walk with Him (spices). Our praises to the Bridegroom are like satisfying spices to His heart.

"I have tasted and enjoyed my wine within you. I have tasted with pleasure my pure milk." Our Lord Jesus has quenched His thirst with the wine of our loving devotion. Even as men run to the feasts of wine to make their hearts glad, Jesus runs to His bride to see our joy and love. The garden within us is where our Lord Jesus is fed and satisfied according to His heart's desire. What we should fully be focused on is our ability to satisfy our Lord, not by serving but by being His spice-filled Eden paradise.

He celebrates all that grace has accomplished in our lives. The Shulamite has given Him all He has desired. *"Wine"* is for celebration and *"milk"* is for strength. This is union and communion in the Holy Place. Our love feast with Jesus brings joy and encouragement to His heart. Are you preparing a feast for your King? Every servant waits until the master eats first, then they are satisfied. So Jesus must first be filled with our praises, gathering His spices, His wine, and His milk—then we are satisfied when we see our praises delight His heart.

Christ is delighted with the sweet offerings of love we give to Him. He gathers them like fruits from a garden, like honey from the honeycomb. Jesus comes to feast on the pure love (*"honeycomb"*) of a mature church. His bride has become nourishment for Him. She asked Him to come and eat; now He has done so. How the Lord is blessed by what the Spirit has done in His bride. Delightful food is being served all over the world as Jesus feasts on our love. Overlooking our faults, He feasts on the love flowing from our hearts.

---

* He does this with His five-fingered hand (Eph. 4:11, i.e., the fivefold ministry).

The garden that satisfies the Savior will also satisfy the nations. Jesus invites His friends to come and eat from the maturity and grace upon the bride: *"Feast on her, my lovers! Drink and drink, and drink again, until you can take no more."* This is absolutely awesome. She has grown from one who neglected her inner life, angered by those who wounded her and consumed with selfishness, to a maturing bride who can be offered to the nations as meat and drink. Jesus wants others to enjoy the fruitfulness of His maturing bridal partner. The bride has become the banquet table for others to feast on the love of the King.

Like the woman at the well, many come to the church and say, "Give me a drink." But they leave thirsty and longing. Would you like to be food for the immature? Would you like to be a drink of refreshing to the parched souls around you? This is what Jesus meant when He said to His disciples who moaned over not having enough bread to feed the five thousand: *"You have the food to feed them"* (Luke 9:13). We run to Jesus for food, but Jesus will one day draw the multitudes to the bride to be fed by love. To the one who was convinced he was a failure, Jesus said, "Peter, feed My sheep."

Jesus brings His friends into His garden to share the fruit of the bride. Those who are beginning in the early stages of holy passion (1:2) are invited in to feast on the maturity of the church that loves Jesus wholeheartedly.* As we allow the Lord to cultivate His garden, to grow His fruit within us, He will take what is His and feed others with it. We then become a true shepherd who feeds the flock. This is how we become shepherds for the immature to follow (1:8).

Pray this prayer today: "Lord Jesus, I love bringing delight to You. Every time You gaze on me, may You find pleasure and joy. Teach me more of what it means to live only and always for You, my Beloved. Give me holy desires today, so that I may live pure and holy, and so that I may reveal to others how wonderful You are. Amen."

---

* Note the parallel of Jacob in Genesis 29:1–10. Jacob becomes a type of Christ who rolls the stone away from his well to water the sheep.

CHAPTER 23

THE SPLENDOR OF THE BRIDEGROOM

**After this I let my devotion slumber,
but my heart for him stayed awake.
I had a dream.
I dreamed of my beloved—
he was coming to me in the darkness of night.
The melody of the man I love awakened me.
I heard his knock at my heart's door
as he pleaded with me... (5:2)**

Spiritual maturity is taking up our cross, following Jesus, and becoming His loving disciples. Wisdom has a cross. Calvary road is a path reserved for every true follower of the Lamb of God. When we embrace the cross, we begin to cherish the things that matter most to Jesus. We become a radiant bride, one whom Jesus will share His life with. Be ready for a fresh vision of the tree of life, the cross of Jesus. Come eat of its fruit.

The Lord Jesus loves to come to us in different forms, imparting new revelation of who He is. This time, He comes not as the sweet Savior or the leaping Prince, but as the Man of Sorrows.

THE SPLENDOR OF THE BRIDEGROOM

We cannot embrace a part of Jesus; we must receive all of Him—the fullness of who He is. Every new season of our lives will bring a new understanding of Jesus, the glorious Son of God. Now a new season has come, a season of testing. The love of her King has accomplished much. She has grown, she has been transformed, but there is still more of Jesus she must discover. After hearing His incredible statements of affirmation, after crying out for the north winds to blow upon her, she falls asleep. Alone in her chamber, she dreams of His approach.

"I let my devotion slumber." Even in her weakness, she couldn't deny her heart: *"But my heart for him stayed awake."* Her heart had been awakened to love. As she lies in bed, the Lord Jesus draws near. She had a dream of her Beloved, and *"the melody of the Man I love awakened me."* Our King comes unannounced in the night seasons to speak His heart to us, awakening us from our slumber.

*"I heard his knock at my heart's door."** The bride is now sensitive to the voice of the Bridegroom. He comes to her, knocking on the door of her heart. It is the voice of the Beloved that knocks on her heart's door. *"He pleaded"* with her, for He longs to take her through a new door in the Spirit (Rev. 3:8, 20). This new door, if opened, will lead to a new revelation of Jesus in her life.

The Bridegroom-King says:

Arise, my love.
Open your heart, my darling, deeper still to me.
Will you receive me this dark night?
There is no one else but you, my friend, my equal.
I need you this night to arise and come be with me.
You are my pure, loyal dove, a perfect partner for me.
My flawless one, will you arise?
For my heaviness and tears are more than I can bear.
I have spent myself for you throughout the dark night. (5:2)

---

* This is *the* Old Testament commentary of Revelation 3:20. Jesus is the heavenly Bridegroom who knocks on the door of the Laodicean church.

Outside the door, knocking, He calls to her with these words: *"Arise, my love. Open your heart, my darling."* There is music in His voice, music that awakens her to the reality of love. Who would not open the door when Jesus draws near singing His song over us? How could we refuse entry to this one who has not one unkind or angry word to speak to our hearts? When He comes knocking on your door, will you open the door and let Him in?

He calls her with four terms of endearment: *"my darling,"* *"my friend,"* *"my equal,"* and *"my flawless one."* * Jesus is the ultimate source of tenderness and compassion. His knock is good; there is nothing to fear when He calls us and stands at the door of our heart knocking. As He looks into the eyes of the maiden, He can see that she is fully His. He calls her His darling, His friend, His equal, and His flawless one. His words of encouragement wash over her, preparing her for the greatest challenge of her life. She has cried for the Spirit winds. She is willing to embrace the cross. Now she is ready for the ultimate test.

"For my heaviness and tears are more than I can bear. I have spent myself for you throughout the dark night." Who is this one coming to her in the middle of the night? This is the Jesus of Gethsemane, the one who lay awake all night long praying for you and for me (John 17; Ps. 22:2; Luke 22:44). He is the one who endured the dark night of the soul and now invites her to join Him in the fellowship of His sufferings (Isa. 53; Phil. 3:10). Jesus is calling her to share His shame, rejection, and loneliness.

This revelation of Jesus is far different than any other the bride has seen thus far. Jesus stands outside knocking, wanting her to embrace the cross, just as He did. We want the Jesus of the banquet table, we want the Jesus who leaps over mountains, but will we embrace the Jesus of Gethsemane? Can we not watch and pray with Him one hour?

---

* Five times in this verse He uses the terms "Me" and "My."

Our Lord Jesus was a Man of Sorrows and was acquainted with grief. It is time for the bride to know His heart, to share His burdens. This was a call to enter into deeper fellowship with the magnificent intercessor. As Jesus struggled in prayer in the garden of Gethsemane, He sweat drops of blood as He faced His agony. Will He find her prepared for this test? The crucified one must have crucified followers.

> **I have already laid aside my own garments for you.**
> **How could I take them up again**
> **since I've yielded my righteousness to yours?**
> **You have cleansed my life and taken me so far.**
> **Isn't that enough? (5:3)**

He had labored all night in prayer and agony while she slept on her bed in comfort. Her response to the knock shows that she is satisfied with what she has experienced thus far. Taking off her robe is the outward work of the cross (taking off her robe of righteousness), a picture of laying aside the old life, but has she truly tasted the cup of His death and sufferings? She has yielded her righteousness to Him. In many translations it says that she has washed her feet by confessing her sins,* but has she inwardly given herself over to death to self and His resurrection life?** Her cry is simply, "Isn't it enough that I have an outward life of goodness?"

Jesus came to disturb her spiritual ease. The Shulamite felt that she had experienced all there was to the cross, but there was more yet to be experienced. God's plan for us is to reveal the cross, deal with us regarding our deep need of Him, and unite us to His death and resurrection. For her to learn these deeper lessons, she must endure the "dark night of the soul," a season where Jesus withdraws from her with no explanation. Can she love Him even while she doesn't sense His presence?

---

* To wash feet is a picture of our outward cleansing through confession and repentance of known sin (John 13).

** Bare feet signify a slave before a master.

Pray this prayer today: "Lord Jesus, I love You when I feel Your presence and I choose to love You when I don't feel that You are near. Help me overcome all my fears and doubts until love wins my every battle. I long for more of You, and I confess that You do all things well. Amen."

CHAPTER 24

THE DOOR OF YOUR HEART

**My beloved reached into me to unlock my heart.
The core of my very being trembled at his touch.
How my soul melted when he spoke to me! (5:4)**

He comes in grace to touch His lover. The heart is that everlasting gateway that swings open to the King (Ps. 24:7). *"The core of my very being trembled at his touch. How my soul melted when he spoke to me!"* This is how the Vulgate, the first Latin translation of the Bible, reads: *"My soul melted when He spoke."* Just one touch from Him and our hearts melt with desire to know Him as He really is. Like the disciples on the road to Emmaus, our hearts burn within us to be close to this lovely one.

The King was trying to get into the room. His touch on the latch opening of her soul caused her to arise and seek Him. She could not stay in bed when He was near. So she says:

**My spirit arose to open for more of his touch.
As I surrendered to him, I began to sense his fragrance—
the fragrance of his suffering love!
It was the sense of myrrh flowing all through me! (5:5)**

She arises in full obedience to open the door to Him. Just as she said yes to the Spirit winds, she now says yes to the Jesus of Gethsemane. But He has gone. As the maiden opens the door for Him, liquid myrrh drips from the door handle. Christ is delighted with the sweet offerings of love we give to Him. He gathers them like fruits from a garden, like honey from the honeycomb. *"I have tasted with pleasure...my honeycomb"* (5:1). Jesus comes to feast on the pure love (honeycomb) of a mature church.

"I began to sense his fragrance—the fragrance of his suffering love. It was the scent of myrrh flowing all through me." The sufferings of her Savior have greatly and ever so powerfully impacted her life. She now carries that same fragrance with her, the fragrance of suffering love flowing through her. This *"flowing myrrh"* points to an abundance of grace that helps us to fully embrace God's will. She is drenched with a desire to walk the way of the cross. The myrrh on the lock was His calling card; the anointing of His sufferings still lingered with her. Somehow, she knew that a baptism of myrrh was ahead.

> **I opened my soul to my beloved, but suddenly he was gone!**
> **And my heart was torn out in longing for him.**
> **I sought his presence, his fragrance,**
> **but could not find him anywhere.**
> **I called out for him, yet he did not answer me.**
> **I will arise and search for him until I find him. (5:6)**

Every sincere believer will someday endure the tests that the Shulamite had to go through. We will not be made mature without the testing of our faith. Most of us do not have a theology that accepts hardships. Because of this, we tend to interpret difficulty as either punishment from God or the direct activity of Satan. Often, however, it is simply God's way of training us and bringing us to the place of maturity. There is no need to bind Satan every time life is rough, nor is it always a sign of God's displeasure with us. Those He loves, He disciplines. The departure of Jesus in this place in the story is *because* she is abandoned to Him, needing the gust of the north wind to blow on her garden to make the fruit sweeter. He has addressed her as one without flaw, His dove.

*"My heart was torn out in longing for Him."** She was moved at the sound of His voice: "Open to Me." Her heart leaped in obedience when He wanted in, but now *"he was gone."* He hides His face from her, so quickly He is gone. It is time now in her journey to understand that God is a God who hides Himself (Ps. 74:11; Prov. 25:2; Isa. 45:15; Hos. 5:6; Luke 22:41).

Immediately she begins to drink of the cup of loneliness and rejection. This is not an attack of the Devil; it is the sovereign purpose of God being worked out in her life. This God-ordained test will move her into Christlikeness. The Gethsemane man is about to teach her about the cross. There is a test from God that is totally unrelated to rebellion. Too often we are like Job's friends who concluded that Job was being afflicted because he was in hidden sin. God will hide His face from the most devout to draw their hearts into pure pursuit, making them wholly His (Job 30:12–31).

During this dark night of the soul,** we can see what is in the deepest parts of our hearts and see our true motives. Jesus told Peter that his faith would be sifted like wheat. Will you be fervent and seek the Lord without the feeling of His presence? Do you pursue Him solely for your own spiritual pleasure, or will you pursue Him for His sake? Can you be faithful regardless of the circumstances you find yourself in?

"I sought his presence, his fragrance." This is a test of major proportions. He cannot be found and He will not answer her cry. Seeking and praying cannot shorten this test; she must experience it fully, embrace every part of it. She throws on her robe and

---

* Or "my heart went out to Him when He spoke."

** Although not found in the Bible, the phrase "dark night of the soul" was used by Catholic contemplatives (i.e., St. John of the Cross) as a term referring to difficult seasons of testing where the believer is seemingly plunged into darkness, needing great faith in God to hold on and overcome.

runs barefoot into the streets looking for her Beloved, *"but could not find him anywhere. I called out for him, yet he did not answer me."* Has this ever happened to you? God will often train us by hiding from us. The silence of a hiding God must do its work in our soul if we are to become mature and complete, which will cause us to mature as we maintain our faith covenant in love even in the silent seasons.

When the Lord withdraws the sense of His presence for a season, we can lose our joy and worship becomes a struggle. We may feel helpless and useless as God seems silent. No amount of pleading brings Him out of hiding. These moments can test us severely, but they can also bring forth fruit that will remain. As we refuse the Devil's voice of accusation, we are able to say with the Shulamite, *"I will arise and search for him until I find Him."*

As I walked throughout the city in search of him,
the overseers stopped me as they made their rounds.
They beat me and bruised me until I could take no more.
They wounded me deeply and removed their covering from me.
(5:7)

Persecution and rejection meet her as the watchmen encountered the confused maiden. The watchmen are those in spiritual authority, the governmental ministries in the body of Christ. She has met the David-type watchmen in 3:3 who are there to help her find a place of deeper intimacy with Jesus, but now the Saul-type watchmen who are motivated by jealousy and fear abuse her.

The watchmen find her. They beat her, bruising her. Their jealousy causes them to discredit those who are in passionate pursuit of Jesus. They find others and begin to wound them with accusations and blame. God has given them a mandate to protect, but instead they use authority in a heavy-handed way to hurt the weak, the stumbling, those struggling in the dark night of their souls. They did not recognize the Shulamite as the bride of the King.

This is a severe test indeed, to be persecuted by those who

should protect. Rising up against her, they take away her cloak (ministry covering) and bruise her cruelly. When those placed over us unjustly persecute us, it brings a wounding that is hard to describe. Mistreatment from friends and leaders is a test that few escape. Even Jesus was wounded in the house of His friends (Ps. 55:12–21).

What is the Shulamite's response to this twofold test of maturity? She has faced the dark night of her soul. Jesus, the Bridegroom, has left her. Only the smell of myrrh dripping from her fingers reminds her that it was more than a dream. Looking for her Lover only left her wounded and bleeding from the mistreatment of leaders. God's presence was withdrawn, and now the body has turned against her. Her covering is removed and she is cast out, losing her place of ministry (although temporarily) in the body of Christ. She cried out for the north winds and they have now come to perfect her faith. He answered her prayer for the north winds because He wanted to expose the unperceived areas of weakness in her heart.

Will you embrace Gethsemane? When everything is gone, can you still serve Jesus with fervent love? Will you continue to love the body when they treat you badly? With all the feelings of pain, hurt, and dishonor, she responds:

Nevertheless, make me this promise, you brides-to-be:
If you find my beloved one,
please tell him I endured all travails for him.
I've been pierced through by love,
and I will not be turned aside! (5:8)

She loves Him no matter what. She is in it for Him. "Yes, You are my passion, Lord. No matter what they do to me; no matter if I can feel You or not—I am lovesick for You." She is not offended at Him for what happened; she is lovesick.

The sorrowing bride wandering in the dark turns to the daughters of Jerusalem, saying, "Tell my Lover that I can't stand it anymore. I love Him more than I can tell, for I am overcome with love! Tell Him I'm not mad. Tell Him I'm not offended at what others have done to me. Tell Him I am faint with love!" The Shulamite has passed the ultimate test—she loves Him still.

The Jerusalem maidens, the brides-to-be, respond, saying:

What love is this?
How could you continue to care so deeply for him?
Isn't there another who could steal away your heart?
We see now your beauty, more beautiful than all the others.
What makes your beloved better than any other?
What is it about him that makes you ask us to promise you this?
(5:9)

Her friends can't understand how she could still love Him so. They can see the strength of her love, but in their amazement they ask, *"Isn't there another who could steal away your heart?"* We don't realize how loudly our faith speaks when we persevere in a time of testing. The immature are strengthened to know our Beloved when they see us faithful in the fires of testing. Just asking this question shows their lack of perception. They cannot understand such devotion during testing. But to her, He has no rival.

The daughters had "other beloveds" that were more important to them than Jesus. The other loves in the lives of believers include people, friends, ministry, money, leisure, pleasure, power, prominence, and comfort. Many born-again people love these things more than Jesus. The definition of spiritual maturity is when Jesus becomes the first and only Beloved of our soul.

The maidens address the Shulamite as *"more beautiful than all the others."* They show a deep respect for this one who has remained loyal, in love with the King. They are able to see His beauty starting to shine upon her. Her godliness, her devotion, and her purity point them to Him. The essence of their question is really, "How can you be so in love with one who treats you like this? Tell us the secret. What is it about your Beloved?" Silence falls on the friends, waiting to see if she will answer...

Pray this prayer today: "Lord Jesus, I refuse to be offended over those who have mistreated me and misunderstood my love for You. I want to be Your partner, always at Your side, never apart. Help me to be faithful to You all the days of my life. Especially today, in whatever I face, to keep You always before me. Amen."

CHAPTER 25

A DREAM

He alone is my beloved.
He shines in dazzling splendor, yet is still so approachable—
without equal as he stands above all others,
waving his banner to myriads. (5:10)

The bride gives the Jerusalem maidens, the brides-to-be, one of the clearest, most glorious descriptions of Jesus Christ found in the Bible. With trembling lips, she begins to tell them about her husband. She has fallen in love with one who has blinded her to all others.

The lovesick bride can never be turned away from the beauty of Jesus. Everything about Him is beyond description. He is altogether lovely. There is none like Him. The twofold test of Jesus hiding from her and the body wounding her has brought her to a new revelation of the splendor of her Bridegroom.

We are about to gaze upon the unveiled glory of the Son of God. The awakened bride gives us a poetic listing of the virtues of Jesus. Once you have seen Him, you cannot draw back from pursuing His presence. Instead of being offended that He had left her for a season, she sets her heart on His beauty and excellence with renewed passion.

You and I must fill our hearts with the revelation of Jesus in our time of testing. Every aspect of His personality has the power to revive and restore your soul when you are under pressure. This is why the Scriptures teach us to *"fasten our gaze onto Jesus"* (Heb. 12:2) when we are tested or burdened. His life is the one life that always pleases the Father. To abide in Him means to draw from these virtues the strength that our weak hearts need.

"He alone is my Beloved." No matter what happens, He is still her Lover. She has kept the fires burning even during the dark night of the soul. There are times it is quite difficult to call Him our Lover when our heart is wounded. The Shulamite is not offended over how He treated her (Matt. 11:6). It is important to let down our guard when we do not understand what He is doing in our circumstances. When we cannot see His face, we can still trust His heart. Call Him your Lover and His brightness will turn the shadows to daybreak. He is completely radiant.

"He shines in dazzling splendor." The words *dazzling splendor* can also be translated as "radiant, sunny, or bright." Even in a time of difficulty and pain, Jesus shines brightly in our night. He is absolutely brilliant in His radiance and stunning in His splendor. What glorious colors surround His throne, for He dwells in abundance of light (1 Tim. 6:16). In appearance, He is compared to the sardius and jasper (Rev. 4:2)—the sardius is deep red in color, while jasper is a transparent green. This radiance speaks of His divine nature, God poured into human flesh.

Many translations use the word *ruddy* to describe Him, which means red or "rosy cheeks." The ruddy nature of Jesus is His human one. Our Lord Jesus is both divine and human; He is *"without equal as He stands above all others,"* outstanding among ten thousand. This speaks of the supremacy and uniqueness of Jesus—there is just no equal to Him (Col. 1:18). It is not hard to see how wonderful He is, for He stands out in a crowd. He is the radiant, shimmering one who is pure and holy. Jesus is incomparably more beautiful and nobler than ten thousand great men combined—He stands above them all (Ps. 45:2; 84:11; Hab. 3:4; Matt. 17:2; Rev. 1:12–18; Dan. 7:9). The number "ten thousand" is the number of infinity. Jesus Christ stands infinitely above all the sons of men. He is the lovely and delightful Prince of Heaven.

> **The way he leads me is divine.**
> **His leadership—so pure and dignified**
> **as he wears his crown of gold.**
> **Upon this crown are letters of black written**
> **on a background of glory. (5:11)**

What follows is a magnificent tenfold description of the Bridegroom. She is now gazing at Him and worshiping Him in the beauty of holiness. She will use the metaphors of the physical body to convey the virtues and glory of the Man Christ Jesus. This is the Ancient of Days, the Creator of heaven and earth. Here are some features about the life and leadership of our King.

Sovereign Leadership

> **His leadership—so pure and dignified**
> **as he wears his crown of gold. (5:11)**

The crown of gold points us to the divine quality of His leadership over us (Dan. 2:32–38; Eph. 1:20–21; Col. 2:10). The highest degree of excellence is found in the leadership traits of our Lord Jesus. There is no leader like Him. There is no mixture in His crown, no impurity. He has crowned us with His wisdom. He leads His flock with compassion and wisdom, strength and mercy.

Jesus is the wisdom of God (1 Cor. 1:30), which is like the finest gold because He has come from the holiest of holies, and on His head are many crowns of gold (Rev. 19:12). His ruling grace combines all the attributes of God in lovely perfection. Blessed are those who have Jesus as their King. In the all-glorious head of gold, the maiden sees the qualities of the headship of Jesus over everything in heaven and on the earth.

Holy Dedication

**Upon his crown are letters of black written
on a background of glory. (5:11)**

Or "His locks are black as a raven." Many Jewish interpreters have seen this phrase as pointing us to the letters of the law written in heaven. Jewish rabbis teach that the precepts of the Word of God (Torah) are written in the heavenly realm, with black letters on top of white flames of glory fire. (Hebrew letters can appear as the locks of hair.)

Jesus was wholly devoted to God. The Nazarite vow forbid one to cut his hair—long hair then becomes a sign of devotion to God. The thick, black, wavy hair was a sign of Jesus's youthfulness, His zeal and vigor (in contrast to balding or gray hair). Jesus is forever young, energetic and zealous in His holy devotion to God and people. He is the same yesterday, today, and forever (Heb. 13:8). His priestly ministry flows from the power of an endless life (Heb. 7:16), and all done with a background of glory! Luke 4:15 says that Jesus taught in the meeting places and He offered everyone glory.

His Loving Insights

**He sees everything with pure understanding.
How beautiful his insights—without distortion.
His eyes rest upon the fullness of the river of revelation,
flowing so clean and pure. (5:12)**

The Shulamite is speaking of the purity of His gaze. A judge may know all the facts about an event, but if his heart is unclean he will not properly interpret them. Jesus's eyes, on the other hand, are clean—eyes that are washed in milk to nourish weak faith and to set in order mixed motives. He can see the sincerity of our hearts, even when our deeds are immature. He is always watching over us and calling us beautiful. He sees every private act of righteousness every time we do not give up under pressure.

He takes note of our positive response to misunderstanding or persecution. He sees the money you've given to His kingdom and His work. And He sees it when you put Him first.

Jesus's eyes speak of His perception, His infinite knowledge, His wisdom and understanding. His eyes are like those of doves. He has singleness of vision and can look upon us with absolute and stunning purity. Even when He sees what is wrong with us, His dove's eyes cover us in love. Like doves by the water streams,* His eyes view us through the cleanliness of divine insight. His discernment of us is untainted or distorted by anger or rejection. He has Holy Spirit anointed vision that is washed in love. His all-seeing eyes detect what is yet to be perfected and brought to maturity.

When we realize that His eyes are full of understanding and revelation, knowing the very deep places of our heart and being, then we don't have to always set the record straight or insist that others understand us. We do this because we know that He understands and knows the full story. We won't feel the compulsion to tell our glory stories or exaggerate what God has helped us to accomplish. Knowing that we are in His gaze day after day is enough.

"How beautiful his insights—without distortion." There is no deformity, no twisted vision. His eyes are sparkling like rare gemstones. There is such beauty in everything about Jesus. The way that He views us with sparkling eyes simply melts our hearts.

His Exquisite Emotions

**Looking at his gentle face I see such fullness of emotion.
Like a lovely garden where fragrant spices grow—
what a man! (5:13)**

Jesus's countenance is always gracious. The emotions of Jesus are like a garden filled with delightful fragrances. His cheeks are

---

* Or "rivers of waters."

windows into His emotional makeup. Everything about Jesus is extraordinary. His emotions are diverse and refreshing.

The Hebrew word for *cheeks* is taken from a root word that means "soft." This means that Jesus is tender of heart. From His heart flowed the kindest of words ever spoken (John 8:11–12). He always gives a soft answer that turns away wrath (Prov. 15:1). *"Fragrant spices"* or "beds of spice" is the Hebrew word *bosem*, which means "creating desire." The life and personality of Jesus awakens the desire within us to know Him.

His Life-Giving Words

**No one speaks words so anointed as this one—
words that both pierce and heal, words like lilies
dripping with myrrh. (5:13)**

His lips were truthful lips (Prov. 12:19). No man has ever spoken like He did (Isa. 50:4), for His lips were anointed with grace (Ps. 45:2; Luke 4:22; John 7:46), and His life was full of prayer and praise. The words from His lips are always life giving and encouraging. His words are Spirit and they are life, every word pure as a lily (John 6:63). The affirming words of Jesus are tender and sweet. His lips kissed heaven in worship and kissed children in compassion. But myrrh was the secret of His anointing.

The myrrh on the speech of Jesus brings people into the revelation of the cross. His words will always exhort us to embrace the cross and die to self. When His Word truly comes to us, it is sharper than any two-edged sword, piercing through our excuses and touching us deeper than any other thing. The lily gives a sweet smell while the myrrh has a sense of suffering attached to it. Both sweetness and boldness can be found on the lips of our King.

His Perfect Power

**See how his hands hold unlimited power!
But he never uses it in anger,
for he is always holy, displaying his glory.
His innermost place is a work of art—so beautiful and bright.
How magnificent and noble is this one—covered in majesty! (5:14)**

The hands of the Lord speak of His power demonstrated in human affairs. His hands are mighty and effective in accomplishing exactly what is in His heart. This power is like rods of gold. The golden rods of power are holy displays of omnipotence. Jesus Christ is the rod of God, the rod of Moses, Aaron's rod that budded in the Holy Place, Isaiah's branch of the Lord, and the Father's scepter of righteousness. Everything God's arm accomplishes is pure and golden, powerful and glorious.

"But he never uses it in anger, for he is always holy, displaying his glory." All the works of Jesus display His glory. His wise skill in all that He does will shine throughout eternity. His deeds display power, but with kindness and goodness. You must discern the beauty in every activity of Jesus in your heart (Rev. 15:4).

Tender Compassion

**His innermost place is a work of art—so beautiful and bright.
How magnificent and noble is this one—covered in majesty! (5:14)**

"His innermost place" can also be translated "His belly" or "His yearning heart." The use of this particular Hebrew word conveys the meaning of tender compassion, a yearning heart (Isa. 63:15; Jer. 31:20). There is no one who enjoys weak people like Jesus. He is the most compassionate and tender one to the failing, struggling believer. Out of His innermost being flow rivers of God's love for thirsty hearts. Clean and bright, this is how He deals with us. His mercy embraces our heart. Jesus is uniquely understanding of the weaknesses of others. Most great people are impatient

with the weaknesses of those under them, yet our King has the rarest of mercies toward all (Exod. 34:6).

"Covered in majesty" can be translated "decorated with sapphires." The sapphire stone is listed as one of the gems attached to Aaron's breastplate, and it is one of the foundation stones of the New Jerusalem (Rev. 21:19). On the sapphire stone the name of Simeon was scratched, which means "he who hears." On the innermost being of Jesus is marked "He who hears." How we rejoice in this one who always hears the Father!

The throne of God is a "sapphire throne" (Ezek. 1:26). In Isaiah 54:11, the loving Bridegroom speaks of the bride (city) as having foundation stones of "sapphires." To mount a sapphire stone into ivory would take time, skill, and creativity. But this is exactly how exquisite the compassion of our Lord is toward us. God's affections are rare, pure, creative, and tender. His love polishes us until we look like sapphires.

His Ways of Wisdom

He's steadfast in all he does.
His ways are the ways of righteousness,
based on truth and holiness. (5:15)

Jesus walks in wisdom beyond measure. His ways (or literally, "His legs") are always executed with strength and dignity. Nothing can stop Him when He is determined to act—His legs are pillars of marble. He does not fail to accomplish what He desires because He bases it all on truth and holiness. He does not waiver under pressure. The dependable ways of our King are like marble rock pillars established in righteousness. Even in her testing, the bride has a pillar to hold her up. Whatever our Lord does, it is based on purity, holiness, and truth (Rev. 15:3; Ps. 25:10). His character is golden from head to toe. The soldiers on Golgotha's hill did not break His legs (John 19:33). The Rock of Ages stands.

His Excellency

**None can rival him,
but all will be amazed by him. (5:15)**

When you gaze at the appearance of our Lover-Friend, it is truly awe-inspiring. Every feature of His countenance, every facet of His wisdom and ways, is colorful and rewarding. "Jesus, You are excellent in every aspect of Your appearance. I love everything about You, Jesus! Beauty streams into our lives when we keep looking at You."

Just looking at Him deposits something virtuous into our lives. His countenance imparts light and joy to our spirits. When we look at His face, it's like looking at the glory of God as seen in the face of Jesus Christ (2 Cor. 4:6), who is the theme and object of our devotion.

His Tender Love

Most sweet are his kisses, even his whispers of love. (5:16)

Jesus is the fulfillment of this sacred journey. Only He can give us sacred intimacy with Himself that is like sweetness to the soul. O, the sweetness of Jesus! He is all delight to my soul. Every pleasure, every source of entertainment and temporary joy, they all fade in comparison to one kiss of sacred intimacy. This is the sweetest, most pleasing experience known to the human spirit. It transforms us over time. It releases an affirmation that lets us soar when times are rough. To know Him is to love Him. To love Him is to be loved by Him. To be loved by Him is heaven. Heaven is the eternal kiss of Jesus Christ.

Pray this prayer: "Lord Jesus, just to think of You overwhelms me. You are beyond description and more than I can comprehend. Enlarge my heart to take in more of You. Open my eyes until I am filled with all the treasures of knowing You. Help me do this, in Your holy name. Amen."

CHAPTER 26

HOLY DESIRE

**He is delightful in every way
and perfect from every viewpoint. (5:16)**

How could we comprehend the intoxicating beauty of our Lord? His love is beyond comprehension, His mercy is above the heavens, His holiness makes mountains melt, and His majesty causes seraphim to cover their faces when in His presence. His affection breaks our hearts. Every beautiful melody, every radiant sunrise, every work of art and beauty, points to Him. Altogether lovely is our Prince and King. Have you ever found anything that is not loveable about Jesus?

In all other beings we see some lack, but in Him there is nothing but perfection. The best of His favored saints have had blots upon their garments and wrinkles upon their brows; but He is nothing but loveliness. All suns have their spots—the fair world itself has its wildernesses; we cannot love the whole of the loveliest thing, but Christ Jesus is gold without alloy, light without darkness, glory without shadows. Yes, He is altogether lovely.

Every aspect of Jesus is radiant and lovely when taken together. Look on Him from whatever position you wish and He is altogether desirable. There is nothing disagreeable or distracting when you gaze upon Him. Every desire of a bride can be found in Him. With delight He satisfies our every longing for a life partner. Nothing else can even be compared to Him. Remember, the Shulamite says all of this without Him near. He has left her for a season, yet her praise and joy is in Him.

If you ask me why I love him so, O brides-to-be,
it's because there is none like him to me.
Everything about him fills me with holy desire!
And now he is my beloved—my friend forever. (5:16)

The words *holy desires* are literally "He is all *desires*." This can also be translated "admirable, graceful, delectable, most pleasant or earnestly desirable." The original word is plural in number, which means Jesus is all *desires*—He is every desire fulfilled. Jesus is all your dreams come true. He is the essence of every delight and pleasure. As every river flows to the ocean and is gathered as one, so Christ becomes to the believer's soul the ocean of all true desires. Jesus is bread to the hungry, water to the thirsty, a garment to the naked, and healing for the wounded. Whatever your soul could desire, Jesus is that and more.

Jesus is altogether lovely simply because of who He is. He is deity dwelling in the flesh, the wonderful and perfect union of God and man. Overflowing with the graces of the Spirit, Jesus becomes the most lovely of all the sons of men. Jesus is altogether lovely as the light to the world, as the way to the Father, and as the truth that sets humanity free. He is the great prophet who brings us back to God, the great high priest to keep us near the heart of our Father, and He is the great King who leads and governs His house with grace and glory.

There is no other friend as openhearted as Jesus. He shares His secrets with us and sympathizes with us in all our failures and weaknesses. He is altogether kind as He feels our sorrows and carries our burdens. He is the lovely Lamb who took away all of our sins. Isn't He wonderful and absolutely stunning?

The question still to be asked of us is this: "Who do you say that I am?"* He is so much more than what we have thought, so much more than what we've been told, so much more than our understanding is able to contain. Altogether lovely, He is without flaw. His garment of righteousness is without seam. All of His perfections flow into unity and wholeness. All the languages of men and angels combined cannot describe how awesome and amazing He is. He is awesome yet playful, affectionate yet terrifying, dancing with us yet breaking our hearts. He is the most tender, yet He is also transcendent. When you have seen Him in His splendor, you could never turn away from Him.

Can you see why the bride could not be offended by the training course she was enduring? The glory of the Bridegroom was infinitely greater than the pain of her process of growth. She calls Him *"my Beloved—my Friend forever."* He is not only the sovereign one, but He is also the one who embraces us as His true friends. What a Savior we have in Jesus!

Listen as the maturing bride speaks of Him with great passion and feeling: *"And now he is my Beloved—my Friend forever."* He is both dearly beloved and a faithful Friend. There is no other friend like Jesus. Never will He disappoint you or walk away when you fail. He is reliable and true. There has never been a husband like Him. She has endured the dark night of the soul without a sense of His nearness. How strong is her love for Him.

"This is my Lover, this is my Friend (5:16)!" Can you see why the bride could not be offended by the training course she was enduring? The glory of the Bridegroom was infinitely greater than the pain of her process of growth. She calls Him "my Beloved" and "my Friend." He is not only the sovereign one whose head is finest gold; He is also the one who embraces us as true friends. What a Savior indeed!

The brides-to-be then ask the Shulamite:

---

* See Matthew 16:15.

O rarest of beauty,
where then has your lover gone?
We long to see him too.
Where may we find him?
We will follow you as you seek after him. (6:1)

The daughters of Jerusalem listened as the maiden extolled the virtues of her Bridegroom. They were spellbound to hear of one so altogether lovely. Now they want to search for Him. In time, they will become the Shulamite of 1:2, and the song will be sung again over them. In 5:9 they asked, *"Who* is He?" But after hearing the bride's glorious description of the Bridegroom, they now question her: *"Where* is He?"

When others see Jesus's beauty, they too will be gripped by holy passion. The goal of all ministry must be to express the splendor of Christ Jesus. The anointed answer of the Shulamite convinced the daughters of Jerusalem that they too must follow after Him. They have to know where they can find Him.

"O rarest of beauty, where has your Lover gone?" Others view the Shulamite as a godly example of the one she follows. The splendor of Jesus has made her beautiful to others. They are using the same phrase that Jesus used to describe her in 1:8. They see her the same way Jesus sees her. Her longing for Jesus above all others has made her life attractive and beautiful, causing them to say, *"We long to see him too. Where may we find him?"* They repeat the question, revealing their earnest longing to know Him the way the bride knows Him. He is still only *her* Lover, not yet *theirs.*

"We will follow you as you seek after him." However, they are convicted of their distance from Him; they must join in pursuit of this King. They want to look for Him alongside of her. We really only find Jesus as we are in fellowship with others rather than in isolation. With a humble and teachable heart, they join together in seeking Him. They are about to become the longing maiden of 1:2 and begin their own sacred journey.

The Shulamite answers their questions:

> **My lover has gone down**
> **into his garden of delight,**
> **the place where his spices grow,**
> **to feast with those pure in heart.**
> **I know we shall find him there. (6:2)**

As she ponders their question, it dawns on her: "I know where He has gone—into His garden! Wait, I am His garden. He is within me!" The garden of the Lord is His church. Jesus is found among His people. This is the lesson repeated throughout the Song of Songs (and throughout the whole of the Bible). We seem to forget in times of testing and spiritual thirst that we can always find Jesus with His people. He loves to hang out with those who love Him. He does not wait until we are perfect before He dwells within us. He waits until we look for Him. He will be with us until the end of the age (Matt. 28:20), and He will love us all the way unto the end (John 13:1).

Beloved, you will find your Friend in His garden, the church. This is the same answer He gave to the Shulamite in 1:8: "Get involved with body life. Follow the tracks of those who follow Me." Your Lover is a gardener who is always involved in making you fruitful and beautiful.

"The place where his spices grow." What different expressions of life can be found in His garden! None of us are the same. We are all like various spices that bring delight to Him when combined. He takes great pleasure in the diversity of His garden, like spice beds of varying flavors. The Lord wants us to value those who are different "spices" (different streams) in His garden. We can be glad that not all churches are like ours. Not all believers are like us.

There is spice in the church for Jesus, for the saints are His special spice beds. The one who created love in us will be delighted in what He sees being produced from our lives. He comes to feed His heart on the variety of our expressions of love toward Him. Jesus loves His whole church, but He will manifest Himself differently to each one with varying levels of intensity.

"To feast with those pure in heart." This speaks of the deep pleasures that come to Jesus from partaking of the love of His bride. His heart feasts on the purity of our devotion to Him. He will go from garden to garden, lampstand to lampstand, seeking those who are pure of heart (Rev. 1:13, 20). He comes to feast with believers who are sincerely devoted to purity, innocence, and bridal loyalty. When Jesus comes to us, He longs to see us united around His fellowship table (the cross) in the same love for each other as we have for Him. And He longs to see purity within our hearts as we do this.

Pray this prayer today: "Lord Jesus, I want to be Your feast of delight, even as I feast on Your love today. My life is complete and full as I live in You. Every desire of my heart is wrapped up into You. Thank You for being my dream come true. I love You, Lord Jesus, with all my heart. Amen."

CHAPTER 27

FULLY HIS

He is within me—I am his garden of delight.
I have him fully and now he fully has me! (6:3)

T his is one of the greatest statements made by the bride in
this narrative. She has heard Him call her His "garden,"
and now she gives herself fully to Him. With new revelation, she is committed to His purpose and His pleasure. Up until
now, she has primarily been seeking Him for *her* pleasure. But
maturity has come. The focus of her life has now turned from self
to the person of Jesus. Her whole life is now His as she is under
His leadership.

To be His bride is to understand that our existence on earth is
for Him. We are not to spend life on our self, but being poured out
for Him, for His glory and His purpose. Her one desire is to be His
inheritance. No one else has any claims on her. She is His and His
alone, shared by none other.

The truth of the matter is that her story is our story, a tran-
sition from a self-centered life to a life that is only His. All of
us begin our journey into the heart of Jesus with the desire to
please ourselves. Our own enjoyment of Jesus is the focus, not
His enjoyment of us. We talk about what Jesus has done for *us* and
what He is to *us*, which is the wonderful joy of knowing Him,
and it is legitimate pleasure. But in time, we must mature in love,

acknowledging His rights to enjoy us. We are Jesus's inheritance. He died to have us.

The thirst of His heart is to commune with His bride and become life itself to each one of us. We exist for Him and His pleasure (Rev. 14:4–5). Blessed are those who unconditionally serve God with no thought of themselves, but are pure in heart. Listen to the words He speaks to her:

O my beloved, you are striking—lovely even in your weakness.
When I see you in your beauty,
I see a radiant city where we will dwell as one.
More pleasing than any pleasure,
more delightful than any delight,
you have ravished my heart,
stealing away my strength to resist you.
Even hosts of angels stand in awe of you. (6:4)

As the maiden speaks with the daughters of Jerusalem, the Lord Jesus suddenly breaks His silence: *"O my beloved, you are striking—even in your weakness."* He praises His bride, communicating His deepest feelings toward her. Remember that He had withdrawn from her (5:2), which brought her out into the dark night to find Him. Jesus had been testing her heart. Now that He has heard her description of Him and her extravagant worship in the midst of His absence, the King praises her using three wonderful metaphors:

When I see you in your beauty,
I see a radiant city where we will dwell as one. (6:4)

The Hebrew text contains the names of two cities, Tirzah and Jerusalem. The name *Tirzah* actually means "beautiful or pleasing," named because of its remarkable natural beauty. Jesus is reaffirming His love for the Shulamite during the season He was distant from her. Using terms of endearment, He compares her heart of loving affection to the natural beauty of the city of

Tirzah. Nine times in the Song of Songs the Bridegroom praises her beauty (two times in 1:15 and 4:1, and one time in 2:10, 2:13, 4:7, 6:4, and 7:7). Never has there been a King like this one who loves His people with an endless love.

Tirzah was the capitol city of the Canaanites before Joshua conquered the land given to the Israelites (Josh. 12:24; 1 Kings 15:33; 16:61). Soon after Solomon's death, a civil war divided the nation of Israel (931 BC). Jeroboam, the king of the northern kingdom, chose Tirzah as his capital city (1 Kings 14:17; 15:21; 16:6) because it was the most beautiful city in the north. It was in the territory of Manasseh's tribe.

The beautiful city of Tirzah becomes a symbolic picture of how the last day's bride of Christ will appear to the unbelieving Gentile nations. The bride will be beautiful to unbelievers and seen as the pleasing partner of Jesus Christ. The unbelievers around us will one day see the work of love accomplished in our personalities.

Jesus declares that the bride is as lovely as Jerusalem, which was the spiritual capital of Israel. It was the city chosen by God for the building of Solomon's temple, which was the only place on earth continually blessed with the manifest presence of God (the *shekinah* glory in the Holy of Holies). God ordained this city as His worship center for the whole world (Isa. 2:1–4; Zech. 14:16–19). Jerusalem's beauty speaks of the beauty of holiness found in worshiping God.

Jerusalem was the capital city of Israel and the joy of the whole earth. God's very presence dwelt over the Holy of Holies in the temple of Jerusalem. The loyal love of the bride is compared to the holy city of Jerusalem, possessing the glory of God. Just as Jerusalem was the center of worship, so the bride's inner beauty is seen by her worship during times of severe testing. This is the real loveliness of her spirit in the fruit of her trials, for she has endured with persevering love. This beauty is what He Himself has perfected in her. His love for us makes us beautiful. Beloved, you are the lovely dwelling place of God.

The Scriptures speak of God's people as a city. We are like a city set on a hill (Matt. 5:13). Abraham looked for this city, whose builder and architect was God, where he looked for two things specifically: a city raised up by God and a bride for his son. John the apostle found them both in the glorified church. When the bride is adorned for her husband, she will come down from heaven as a city (Rev. 21). The New Jerusalem is not merely a place, but a people. The bridal community, *"the radiant city,"* that God will establish on the earth someday will be those who are adorned with His beauty.

**You have ravished my heart,
stealing away my strength to resist you.
Even hosts of angels stand in awe of you. (6:4)**

The Shulamite has walked through her season of testing with victory. Her loyalty has made it impossible for Him to resist her, so that she ravishes His heart. She has remained loyal to Him no matter what. And Jesus says that even the angels stand in awe of what she has become. She has become His victorious bride and the banner of love (2:4) and has become her banner of victory in times of affliction.

These words must sink deeply into your life. You have the ability to ravish the heart of Jesus. You cause His heart to skip a beat when you come before Him to pour out your abandoned worship at His feet. Nothing moves His heart more than you do. Keep coming to Him when you are weak and even when you cannot feel His presence. Keep coming to worship Him because of how it moves His heart. Never withhold from Jesus what means the most to Him—your worship.

Pray this prayer today: "Lord Jesus, my love for You is growing and overtaking me. I want You to know how much I adore all that You are and all that You have done inside of me. I long to love You more. Enflame my heart with holy passion as I pursue You in my sacred journey. Amen."

CHAPTER 28

JESUS OVERWHELMED

Turn your eyes from me; I can't take it anymore!
I can't resist the passion of these eyes that I adore.
Overpowered by a glance, my ravished heart—undone.
Held captive by your love, I am truly overcome!
For your undying devotion to me is the most yielded sacrifice. (6:5)

How can it be that Jesus sees His bride with such compassion? We are lovely in His sight. When we pursue Him in the midst of our pain with loyal love, His heart is moved beyond description. He tells the worshiping bride to stop gazing at Him: *"I can't take it anymore!"* Beloved, when your eyes of faith are fixed on Him, do you know what that does to Jesus? Your look of love overwhelms His heart. Your eyes of faith prevail over the Son of God. This is why He says, *"Turn your eyes from me, I can't take it anymore! I can't resist the passion of the eyes that I adore."*

The Shulamite has been sifted like wheat, tested over and over again, and all this time she didn't even have a clue that her devotion was irresistibly beautiful to the King. So He uses poetic language, asking her to turn away her gaze. Jesus could not withstand her ceaseless adoration anymore than one man could withstand an army coming against him. This is the great power of your love and affection that is lavished on the Son of God.

What is so ravishing about the sight of this bride that it overwhelms God the Son? What would He see in us that would make Him say, *"I am truly overcome"*? It is the sight of holiness and purity that has prepared us to rule now with Him, to sit where He dwells as His regal partner. The beauty of His glory is streaming from the inner being of His partner bride, and it conquers His heart. It is time for *you* to see yourself as a ravishing sight of beauty and virtue in His eyes.

When the church, the bride, actually manifests the fullness of what love has deposited within us, we will overcome our Beloved, winning His heart. You truly have hold of the heart of your Lover-Friend when you worship with endless praise. Imagine that your flashing eyes of fiery love overwhelm the mighty Son of God, the Prince of Glory. Your beautiful devotion overcomes His heart. The eternal Bridegroom declares Himself "defeated" by the bride. She has defeated Him with dove's eyes.

The bride is still not perfect yet, and neither are you. She has yet to come out of her wilderness leaning on the Beloved, yet she still has the capacity to ravish the heart of God. One of the great revelations of the Song of Songs is that even weak and incomplete believers overwhelm the heart of God as they turn to Him with real love.

Jesus made the entire universe—the stars, the Milky Way, the constellations, the sky, fields, and mountain peaks—yet none of creation's beauty overwhelms Him like you. This eternal King will one day lift up a rod of iron over the nations and use it to crush them to pieces. All of Satan's fury will come against the coming King in the day of His splendor. Even while no one can conquer or overcome Him, your glance of love leaves Him undone.

"Your undying devotion to me is the most yielded sacrifice." Can you see what your enduring faithfulness to Jesus does to Him? Your love for Him in the midst of testing is more precious to

the Bridegroom than you can take in. This ultimate warrior is so easily conquered by the devotion of His wife. Your eyes of passion are stronger than the Lord Jesus Christ. Every passionate, love-filled worshiper has power to move the heart of the King. The charm of your eyes is unbearable to the Bridegroom. Just a glance and you conquer Him. This is why Christians are called more than conquerors—they are conquerors of the one who overcomes all.

The shining of your spirit shows how you have taken my truth to become balanced and complete.
Your beautiful blushing cheeks
reveal how real your passion is for me,
even hidden behind your veil of humility. (6:6–7)

The bride has grown from an immature maiden who didn't have a clue as to what the King had prepared for her, to a strong and devoted bride. Her cheeks reveal His unchanging love and her unwavering devotion to God. This is true love, face-to-face.

Her ministry fruitfulness comes from her life in the Word. Her "teeth" bearing twins speaks of a double portion of fruitfulness. She is compared to the sheep in which none are barren. The sheep in this passage are both clean and fruitful due to their life in the Word (John 15:7–8). A diligent life in the Word guarantees fruitfulness (1 Tim. 4:6–16).

Every feature of the Shulamite speaks of her growth in God. Hearing His words, gazing upon Him, and spending time in His presence has been the secret to her maturity. There is something so powerful, so alluring about our Jesus—just being in His presence will radically change us deeply and forever. Think about this again: Jesus sees beauty in us. When He could point out our failures, our incomplete obedience, our immaturity and weakness, He points to our virtues. This is our Bridegroom, the one we serve with a whole heart.

**I could have chosen any from among the vast multitude
of royal ones who follow me.
But one is my beloved dove—unrivaled in your beauty,
without equal, beyond compare,
the perfect one, the only one for me.
Others see your beauty and sing of your joy.
Brides and queens chant your praise:
"How blessed is she!" (6:8–9)**

The bride is preeminent in honor among the vast multitude in Jesus's court. Jesus proclaims that no one compares to the passionate bride. None, not even the glorious angelic hosts who do His bidding. There is absolutely no one in all of creation who is as preeminent as her.

In the book of Esther, there were many in the harem of the king, but the queen was distinguished above all others. The full intimacy and authority before this King is reserved for only one— the Shulamite. There may be many in the King's courts, but she alone is His dove, His perfect one, unique above all others. The love of Jesus is so powerful that He can look at each one who pursues Him and say that they are without equal.

Unrivaled in your beauty without equal, beyond compare... (6:9)

Can you imagine the Son of God looking at you with your failures, calling you *"unrivaled in your beauty"*? Love has made you lovely. Redemption has given you the robe of righteousness. You are perfected for all time through the blood of Christ (Heb. 10:14). The perfection of the Shulamite is in her undefiled love of her Bridegroom. She is His magnificent obsession; He wants no other but her. Of all the glorious hosts in Jesus's courts in the eternal city, He has only one bride.

She is unique, unrivaled. She has no competition. Jesus is saying, "Of all the attendants in My court, she is the only one I want and the only one I would die for." Jesus is saying to her what she said to Him in 5:10 and 16, that she is unique and has captured His heart. She is the chief among ten thousand in His heart, as is He in her heart. He wants no other. For she is the favorite, *"without equal, beyond compare,"* the perfect one, the only one for Him.

**Look at you now—
arising as the dayspring of the dawn, fair as the shining moon.
Bright and brilliant as the sun in all its strength.
Astonishing to behold as a majestic army
waving banners of victory. (6:10)**

All the immature believers marvel at the grace and dignity of the bride. The grace upon her is attractive, bringing the praise of many. This is how the bride will one day be seen. Spiritual maturity will be seen as glorious, not a legalistic denial or fanaticism. As the saints and angels marvel at God's wisdom manifest in the church, all jealousy will be removed.

It is a testimony of light and glory upon those who have been in deep spiritual communion with the Lord in His Holy Place. This is the Holy Spirit pointing to the uncommon beauty of the bride, comparing her to the celestial objects. No longer a ragged goat-keeper, she is now a radiant bride. Here is the fourfold description of the one Jesus has transformed:

1. *"Arising as the dayspring of the dawn."* The morning light that brings hope is rising upon the church. In chapter 2 she was looking *for* the morning, but now she is looking *like* the morning! The dawn signals a new beginning, a new start in the things of God. With fresh mercy, the church reaches out to the new day of His appearing (Ps. 130:1–3; Lam. 3:22–23). She shines forth and appears like the dayspring of the dawn, which is a picture of endtime glory rising upon us.

Just as a sunrise begins slowly, brightening the eastern sky, so the spiritual growth of each passionate follower of Jesus occurs gradually (Prov. 4:18). She had proclaimed, *"Until the daysprings to life and the shifting shadows of fear disappear (2:17),"* now it is happening. The shadows of compromise are leaving her as a new day of voluntary love begins.

2. *"Fair as the shining moon,"* or as *"beautiful as the full moon"* (NASB). There's a full moon rising. The church is seen in Scripture as the moon, reflecting the light of the Son. Ordained by God to give light to the world (Gen. 1:14–19), the church also reflects the light of Christ for a darkened planet (Phil. 2:15). All of our beauty comes from Jesus Christ.

As a reflection of our Bridegroom, the church shines through the night season of His absence. Although marred by the craters of our sin, we shine, enduring the attacks of Satan, ruling during the night seasons. The faithful witness of the full harvest moon speaks of our power to evangelize (Ps. 89:37; Matt. 5:16). Twelve times a year the moon gives forth her testimony—twelve is the number of divine government. Therefore, the church will reflect God's light as the reality of the New Jerusalem, the eternal city, consumes us. Having the glory of God, our reflected light, will be like a most precious stone, like a jasper stone, clear as crystal (Rev. 21:11).

3. *"Bright and brilliant as the sun in all its strength."* The increasing greatness of His glory is shining upon her. First, the dim rays of sunrise appear, then the beauty of a full harvest moon, and now she shines as clear as the sun. From glory to glory God will take us, until we carry the image of Jesus. God loves the Son so much that He will fill heaven with people just like Him.

We will someday be as *"bright as the sun."* Deborah, the prophetess, spoke of a day when those who love the Lord would shine like the sun *"when it rises in its strength"* (Judg. 5:31, NIV). Jesus also spoke of a day when the *"righteous will shine like the sun in the kingdom of their Father"* (Matt. 13:43, NIV). Jesus is the "sun" of the celestial city (Rev. 21:23), of which the "sun of righteousness" will be the light. Only the church is described with the same metaphor as the Lord Jesus (Rev. 12:1). As queen of the night and the day, and queen of the new heavens and new earth, the bride will carry His glory throughout eternity. She has now become a mirror that reflects the beauty of the Lord.

4. *"Astonishing to behold as a majestic army waving banners of victory."* The militant church is about to arise, awesome as an army with banners. The majestic army will experience total victory over every dark foe. As she triumphs over all sin, she becomes God's "war club" (Jer. 50:20). The church is about to be transformed into a wonderful army of victory, waving our flags. These banners we wave are the virtues of the one we love. We wave the banner of love, the banner of forgiveness, and the banner of endless hope. Our banners enable us to overcome as we dance to their truths. We will push back forces of darkness with waving banners of triumph.

How glorious is the love of God! We have come so far in this journey. Once we were wayward and lost in darkness, but now He has made us bright and dazzling. What a holy injustice, to take former rebels and enthrone them on high. The Lord delights in giving His church His glory. What looks first like a sunrise on the horizon will one day light up the eternal city—this is the advancing church.

Pray this prayer today: "Lord Jesus, I love to love You! I want to be a shining one, radiant with Your glory, full of faithful love toward You. Empower me to arise and shine with the light of love. I give You all my heart, and I thank You that You live in me. Amen."

CHAPTER 29

HIS CHERISHED COMPANION

I decided to go down to the valley streams
where the orchards of the king grow and mature.
I longed to know if hearts were opening.
And the budding vines blooming with new growth?
Has their springtime of passionate love arrived? (6:11)

The bride is now beginning to see her destiny. She has said yes to full obedience, whatever the cost, even while enduring the north winds of adversity. The Lord has shown her the unperceived fault lines beneath the surface of her life. As the cherished companion of Christ, she has received the fourfold testimony of the Lord (6:10). Now she is ready to turn toward the body of Christ and be a blessing to others. A mature love for the church has grown within the maiden.

In the past, persecution and the immaturity of others have wounded her, but now she has changed. Philippians 2:3–4 is becoming a reality to her—she is ready to live for others: *"Each of you should look not only to your own interests, but also to the interests of others."*

The *"orchards"* are actually the "grove of nut trees."* What a humorous description of the church this is! We always knew there were "nuts" in the church. She humbles herself to *"go down"* and look at the places where the orchards grow and have "new growth" birthing other ministries. She goes down to the valley streams, not only to look but also to intercede for others.

These ministries are compared to walnut trees. Just like a walnut, many of us have hard shells that must fall to the ground and die before the fruit will appear (John 12:24). The walnut was once used both for soap and for food, which speaks to cleansing and nourishment for others. Providing shade, these trees would someday become a source of refreshing for many. The maiden comes humbly and willingly to affirm and intercede for the growing ministries in the body of Christ. Her self-consumed attitude is being replaced with true servanthood in the church.

Notice that the new growth is found near the *"valley streams."* The low places of life are really the places of great fertility, as the fruit of Christlikeness is brought forth out of our valleys. She too found her growth in the valley (2:1), and so now she is willing to run and bless the others who are maturing through the experiences of living in the valley as well. *"Budding vines"* speak of the maturing stages of ministries—first the new growth, then the buds, and then afterward the fruit.

The Shulamite is no longer critical of the immaturity of other ministries; she is quick to recognize their strengths, their growth, and potential for fruitfulness. Every maturing saint will embrace the *"budding vines"* of ministries that are immature or limited in some way. How prone we are to exalt ourselves! Those who have been humbled by the Spirit will always see new growth, not just old wounds.

---

* The garden or grove of God is mentioned nine times in the Song of Songs. The first three references are to *her* garden (4:12, 15–16), while the last six references are to *His* garden (4:16; 5:1; 6:2, 11; 7:12; 8:13).

It is wrong to despise the ministries of others. Paul pronounced blessing on other ministries that criticized and condemned him (Phil. 1:15–18). The Holy Spirit will not allow us to be impatient with others, despising their immaturity. An unrelenting gratitude will fill the heart of the radiant bride. We cannot be impatient with others when we remember our own history. God is raising up a people who will love and embrace the entire body of Christ, not only those we are comfortable with but the entire body in all her diversity.

Many are disgusted with the "budding vines" of ministries that are different, perhaps even abrasive to our unbroken flesh. But in every immature ministry (and every immature believer) there are virtues that are just beginning to bud. Filled with love for others, we can weep like Joseph over our brothers who wounded us in their ignorance (Gen. 50:15–21). Her passion to make Him known to others sweeps her off her feet:

> **Then suddenly my longings transported me.**
> **My divine desire brought me next to my beloved prince,**
> **sitting with him in his royal chariot.**
> **We were lifted up together! (6:12)**

Before the Shulamite realizes it, her intercession lifts her up in ecstatic joy and sets her next to Him in His royal chariot, the glorious royal chariot. This depicts the zeal she feels for others. The bride's soul moved like a chariot. In the ancient world, a chariot was the fastest and easiest way to travel with luggage over long distances. The best chariots belonged to the noble people or the royal family. The chariot of God is swift and powerful, transporting the soul.

Another translation of "royal chariot" is "the chariot of Ammi-nadib." Some scholars believe Ammi-nadib was the name of one of Solomon's celebrated chariot drivers. Ancient Jewish interpreters translated this as "the chariot of my willing, princely people." She is caught up into the delights of the spiritual realm through her fervent intercession. Her soul was made like the King's chariot that moved swiftly.

In other words, the Shulamite suddenly found strong desires and enthusiasm moving across her soul to serve God's people. Mature love has broken through. She is in a place of intensity and zeal for God to move among others. The spirit of intercession has fallen upon her. She is taken away and caught up into a new realm of passion for the people of God. She is beside herself, compelled by love (2 Cor. 5:11, 14). Instead of being put off by the immaturity, pride, wrong applications of the Word, and lack of discernment of these *"budding vines,"* she is now surprised by the tender compassion that she feels.

God loves the whole church, not just the part we are involved in. He wants us to have ownership of the whole church, not just the small part under our authority. Zeal for the entire church is foundational to the unity of the body of Christ (John 17:21). Most only support what is theirs, or what they identify with the closest. The Lord is raising up shepherds who care about His larger purposes and who train the people to love the whole church. She is filled with love for the body, like Joseph was for his brothers, without any sense of bitterness over the way she was mistreated (Gen. 50:15–21).

Listen to the words of the brides-to-be as they witness the beauty and symphony of the dance of the Shulamite:

Come back! Return to us, O maiden of his majesty.
Dance for us as we gaze upon your beauty. (6:13)

The maiden has left to go to the Lord's garden and bless others. The sincere daughters cry out four times *"Come back,"* showing the intensity of their desire to be near her. Mature saints are the glorious ones, the truly attractive ones to others in the body of Christ. For those with immature faith, it is sometimes easier to see Jesus through the mature saints. She has released the fragrance of Christ among them. They long to have her example in their midst. They see her love for the weak, immature, struggling believers and wish for her to stay and impart more of her mature love to them. This is similar to Paul leaving the Ephesian elders in Acts 20:15–38. They too wept as Paul was taken from them to fulfill his destiny. How beautiful is this bride.

The Shulamite bride responds:

> **Why would you seek a mere Shulamite like me?**
> **Why would you want to see my dance of love? (6:13)**

She is called the *"Shulamite"* because she grew up in the Israelite city of Shunem. This is the only place in the song in which the bride is called the Shulamite. *Solomon* and *Shunem* come from the same root word, which means peace. Jesus and His bride have the same name.

Now, the beloved Shulamite bride speaks to the sincere daughters, the Shulamites-to-be. The bride asks those gazing on her this question: *"Why would you seek a mere Shulamite like me? Why would you want to see my dance of love?"* She's asking, "What do you see in me? Is it like watching the dance of angels?" The soon-to-be Shulamites will answer this question in chapter 7.

The Shulamite bride's dance of love is similar to the dance of Mahanaim, the dance of angels. Mahanaim was the place where Jacob was left alone as he waited for his older brother, Esau. They had quarreled years earlier when Jacob deceived his father and brother, stealing the birthright through trickery. It was at Mahanaim that Esau pursued Jacob. It was also here that Jacob encountered two companies of angels, which is why he named it Mahanaim ("two camps" or "two armies").

Mahanaim is the place where angels dance over the one who returns to his or her destiny. The angels of the Promised Land formed a welcoming committee to bless Jacob as he returned to his inheritance. Jacob was the Old Testament prodigal son who was coming back to his father's house of promise. The angels encircled Jacob and danced for joy over his return. It is the dance of unbridled passion and celebration.

The Bridegroom-King speaks now and answers the question posed by the Shulamite:

**Because you dance so gracefully,
as though you danced with angels! (6:13)**

These two camps of powerful angels would provide Jacob's protection from his angry brother. Jesus refers to the dance of angels as He gazes upon His radiant bride as well. Just as Jacob saw this dance as he returned to the Promised Land, so the bride is dancing with angels as she begins to walk in the fullness of her inheritance. Truly she is beautiful in His eyes, for she is now like one dancing in victory with the angelic hosts. She has conquered Him with a glance; now she may dance with Him. What a beautiful song to dance to!

Pray this prayer today: "Lord Jesus, truly I am beautiful in Your eyes. I am starting to see the destiny You have for me and I say yes to obeying You completely, no matter the cost. Mature my love for those around me so I can love them as You love them. We are all a part of Your radiant bride. Shine upon us, Jesus. Amen."

CHAPTER 30

DELIGHTED WITH HER BEAUTY

How beautiful on the mountains
are the sandaled feet of this one bringing such good news.
You are truly royalty!
The way you walk so gracefully in my ways displays such dignity.
You are truly the poetry of God—his very handiwork.
Out of your innermost being is flowing the fullness of my Spirit—
never failing to satisfy.
Within your womb there is a birthing of harvest wheat;
they are the sons and daughters
nurtured by the purity you impart.
How gracious you have become!
Your life stands tall as a tower, like a shining light on a hill.
Your revelation eyes are pure,
like pools of refreshing—sparkling light for a multitude.
Such discernment surrounds you,
protecting you from the enemy's advance.
Redeeming love crowns you as royalty.
Your thoughts are full of life, wisdom, and virtue.
Even a king is held captive by your beauty. (7:1–5)

As Jesus comes forth in His church, He will turn our hearts to the poor of the earth. The nations must know Him. Passion for Jesus will eventually bring us to the place of serving others. Revival will transform the vision and destiny of the church. Jesus is a prophet whose words will come to pass.

The maiden gave a tenfold description of the glory of the Bridegroom (5:10–16), now the King gives a tenfold prophetic declaration over His bride. What tenderness is in the heart of this King. Her beauty has completely captivated Him. He is releasing more and more of His life and beauty to her. She is reflecting the qualities of His endless life.

These ten prophecies will be fulfilled in the church before Jesus returns. They are descriptions of virtues and strengths that He will supernaturally deposit within her. Essentially, what follows is a practical definition of godliness and virtue that will arise like a shining light within the church.

This is the second time the King describes the bride in detail. In 4:1–5, He gave eight affirmations beginning with her head; here He now gives ten affirmations beginning with her feet. These prophecies are meant to be a practical challenge to our growth in God.

In what follows God is giving us a prophetic roadmap for spiritual growth coming to the end-time bride. These prophetic virtues will be seen in her as the church gives herself to bridal passion in pursuit of the Son of God. Ask God to give you these attributes today. Let them become fuel for your intercession. Cry out for your life and for your church to manifest these traits.

Her Good News Shoes

How beautiful on the mountains
are the sandaled feet of this one bringing such good news. (7:1)

Beautiful feet in sandals speak of evangelism. Paul wrote to the Ephesians about the church whose feet were shod with readiness to preach the gospel of peace (Eph. 6:15). The maiden is now swift to take the gospel to others. A spirit of evangelism is flowing in the church: *"How beautiful on the mountains are the feet of those who bring good news, who proclaim peace"* (Isa. 52:7, NIV).

It is our inheritance to evangelize and claim spiritual territory with the soles of our feet (Josh. 1:3). Winning souls to Jesus Christ will be the joy and delight of the bride as she begins to shine as a burning lamp for the nations. She had taken off her shoes in 5:3, and now she is wearing the beautiful sandals of reaching the lost. O, the beautiful, dancing feet of the Shulamite!

Her feet are not bare, as a beggar's. She has the "good news shoes" upon her feet, shoes that can walk upon the rocky hearts of humanity in evangelism. This is the church in militant victory, clothed with the wardrobe of warfare. Evangelism is a form of spiritual warfare, as we tear down strongholds of unbelief and false religion in the hearts of humanity. The gospel is the power of God to bring deliverance and freedom to the lost (Rom. 1:16).

"How beautiful." The church will be powerful and successful in evangelism as the bride flows as one with the Bridegroom. Her labors will be fruitful as the anointing of the Bridegroom is seen upon the mature bride. She is in love with the King. This makes her beautiful to the nations. Someday they will all see the beauty of the Lord Jesus upon the feet of those who are swift to speak of Him. She is the daughter of the Prince of Glory. She is the princess bride. With royal grace she moves out to win the nations and shine the light of Christ upon every dark corner of the earth. By the new birth, she is linked in spirit and in virtue to the Prince. Everyone can see it now.

Her Graceful Walk

The way you walk so gracefully in my ways displays such dignity.
(7:1)

This could also be translated as "your graceful legs are like jewels." The declaration over her is that she walks *"so gracefully"* and with *"such dignity,"* the dignity of the one who loves her and gave Himself for her. She's walking in His power and grace as through the disciplines of the Spirit she has developed the walk of a queen. She is fully ready to sit at His side.

You are truly the poetry of God—his very handiwork. (7:1)

Jesus is the skilled poet! He's formed us, shaped us, made us, broken us, healed us, and filled us. He knows us inside and out, and is aptly qualified to write a song about us. The touch of His finger has touched our thigh as it did with Jacob. Even with "Jacob's limp," we are still God's beautiful poetry (Eph. 2:10). As the master poet, He has written the rhymes of heaven upon our human spirit. The entire universe will one day see His divine handiwork in the church.

The love of our King has strengthened us and prepared us for end-time ministry. The church will broadcast His walk of wisdom and power. Our lives have been charted out ahead of time. Our God is not a haphazard sovereign; He has purposefully shaped our walk to fulfill the destiny He has chosen for us (Eph. 2:8–10; 3:9–11).

Her Inward Life

Out of your innermost being is flowing the fullness of my Spirit—never failing to satisfy. (7:2–3)

The Shulamite's innermost being speaks of her inner life. This inner life is the result of her attachment to the life and Spirit of the Lord. Her innermost being is flowing with rivers of living water (John 7:37–39). Her life in the Spirit is rich, abundant, overflowing, never lacking, and *"never failing to satisfy."* A fountain has opened up within her. This prophecy will be seen as the church is connected to Christ and flows in the fullness of His Spirit.

This ever-flowing *"fullness of* [His] *Spirit"* is often translated as "blended wine," which speaks of balance and the full-range of nourishment she's giving to the nations. Maturity in her inner life brings a satisfaction of fullness to the thirsty hearts around her. Are you one who overflows with rivers of refreshment to others? So often we drain life from others instead of giving it. "Lord, make us Your goblet of blended wine for the joy of others."

Giving Birth to a Harvest

Within your womb there is a birthing of harvest wheat (7:2-3)

Harvest wheat in Scripture is a vivid picture of the coming harvest of souls. This is a prophetic declaration that a great harvest is soon coming through the church. From the womb of the mature bride comes a harvest of wheat, not tares. Like a pregnant belly, the bride is beginning to show. She has been eating the hidden manna of Revelation 2:17, so she is bread for the nations as the harvest bursts forth from her inner life. Wheat also points us to the bread of God, the words of eternal life (John 6:33, 51, 68). This incredible harvest will be set about with holiness, bridal love, purity of heart, and passion for Jesus.

Her Power to Nurture Others

**They are the sons and daughters
nurtured by the purity you impart. (7:2-3)**

With an inner beauty of purity the Shulamite is able to nurture and edify the young ones. She not only gives birth, but she will love and care for the young ones, nurturing babes by the milk of the Word of God. She has been prepared to birth a harvest as well as bless those she wins to Christ. She will raise up sons and daughters who are able to replicate the very works of the Lord of glory and are established in grace and purity. Although the Hebrew text contains the words "your breasts," it is speaking metaphorically of her ability to nurse the rising generation with the "milk" or pure, unadulterated truth.

Her Determination

**Your life stands as tall as a tower,
like a shining light on a hill. (7:4)**

This first phrase could also be translated as "your neck is like an ivory tower." In 4:4 the Bridegroom described her *"as secure as David's fortress,"* but now He says that her *"life stands as tall as a tower."* A tower speaks of protection and uprightness. She will pay the price for being tall and beautiful in the sight of the nations. Furthermore, she will stand *"like a shining light on a hill."* As a lighthouse she will shine the light of Jesus to the nations. And a tower is a word picture of her resolute determination that has become her protection from evil. She has become a strong refuge for others against the enemy.

Her Clear Revelation

Your revelation eyes are pure, like pools of refreshing— sparkling light for a multitude. (7:4)

The eyes of her understanding have been enlightened in answer to the apostolic prayer of Ephesians 1. Her faith and revelation have grown; pure spiritual insight characterizes her life. Beloved, the church of Jesus Christ will soon walk in the light of Christ and in the knowledge of His ways. Her dove's eyes have now become *"pools of refreshing."*

The Hebrew text is actually "like the pools of Heshbon." These pools were known as some of the cleanest pools in the land. The city of Heshbon was the royal city of the Amorite king, Sihon (Num. 21:25–26). The bride's vision and revelation in the Spirit are pure; her insights can be trusted. The words she speaks to others are timely and refreshing. No longer like muddy pools, her discernment has been cleansed of the flesh. Her spiritual vision is a reservoir of revelation. She will make her judgments based on the love revelation the Bridegroom gives her, not from a heart of impurity. *Heshbon* can also mean "stronghold." She spoils the kingdom of darkness with her knowledge of the Lord.

And the Hebrew text adds: "By the gate of Bath Rabbimm," which means "the unique daughter among many." As the multitude of nations looks into the eyes of the radiant bride, they will see pure revelation, grace and deep calm. Many will drink from her pools of revelation formed by her intimate experience of knowing the King in His fullness.

Her Spiritual Discernment

**Such discernment surrounds you,
protecting you from the enemy's advance. (7:4)**

She has the ability to "sniff out" the enemy and know where he is at work. The Shulamite has grown in her discernment and is effective in spiritual warfare. Her supernatural discernment in spiritual warfare will be the source of protection from the schemes of the enemy. Without a keen discernment, we are all vulnerable to the strategies of darkness. This knowledge is not logic, subject to human reasoning, but spiritual discernment based on the Word of God. It transcends what is heard or seen and will differentiate between what is from man, God, and the Devil. Precise battle plans will be granted to the seeking, sensitive bride. Jesus will have a bride who is alert, giving protection to the nations.

Her Pure Thoughts

Redeeming love crowns you as royalty. (7:5)

Or it could be translated as "your head crowns you like Mount Carmel." The crowned head speaks of our thoughts and wisdom that bring either disgrace or beauty. The bride has purity of thought and excellence of wisdom. What grace is upon her! She is quick to bring her thoughts into the obedience of Christ as she tears down strongholds. The helmet of salvation and deliverance is upon her head like a crown. Filled with hope, she does battle against every high thought that opposes the wisdom of God (2 Cor. 10:1–5).

In the Hebrew text, her thoughts were compared to "Mount Carmel." Mount Carmel was considered one of the most excellent and beautiful peaks in the land. The Shulamite's fruitful wisdom and purity of thought can now be compared to this mountain. Carmel can mean "fruitful field." Her thoughts are fruitful—full of life, wisdom, and virtue. The thoughts of the bride are victorious, like Mount Carmel, which was the place that God sent fire as an answer to Elijah's prayer. Redeeming love is her royal crown. Her crowns speak of dominion and power over her foes. Once she was a captive, but now she is royalty, crowned with His redeeming love.

Her Dedication to Jesus

Your thoughts are full of life, wisdom, and virtue.
Even a king is held captive by your beauty. (7:5)

The royal heart of abandoned love fills her in her dedication to Him. Her thoughts are full of life, wisdom, and virtue. The devotion of her life to the King is so unmistakable that even the angels are in awe of this one shining like the sun. She comes forth from her trials, unshakable in her consecration to heaven's Christ.

Can you imagine the King of Glory being held captive as He gazes on the Shulamite bride and the depth of devotion coming from her heart? In the face of her resolve to do the will of God, no matter what it costs her, Jesus is filled with delight and affection. He is overcome, held captive, imprisoned in her love! Your love captures the King. You are why He died on the cross. It is the joy of our Lord to be captivated in holy love for His bride.

Like Jacob clinging to the wrestling man, her heart clings to the Bridegroom, until undying love prevails over His heart and holds Him captive. She is all He can think about. They are meant to be together forever, bride and Bridegroom held in each other's embrace. No more foxes to spoil the vines, no hidden compromise, and no unwillingness to arise when He calls her. She's filled with royal love for the King. Jesus will have a bride who is as devoted to Him as He is to the Father.

Pray this prayer today: "Jesus, Your words of love over me are more than I can take in. Help me to receive the depths of Your love. Overwhelm me in Your love. Baptize me in the might of Your love until every distraction of my life becomes nothing at all compared to the intensity of Your love. Amen."

CHAPTER 31

PLEASING TO THE SON OF GOD

**How delicious is your fair beauty;
it cannot be described as I count the delights you bring to me.
Love has become the greatest. (7:6)**

The graceful, dancing, radiant bride. Look at her as she arises to embrace the Bridegroom who is a King. Beautiful, pleasant, delightful, pleasing—she is being conformed into the image of the one she loves so fervently. Love has transformed her heart. He is completely satisfied with the many glories of His own nature coming forth from within her (Isa. 62:4; Zeph. 3:16–17; Mal. 3:12). Jesus lifts His song to a higher key and rejoices over her with singing. He uses the same words she spoke over Him to describe how He sees her. How can you take in the depths of His love?

The Lord so enjoys the fruits of bridal love and obedience from you and me. It is a pleasure to Him beyond our understanding. The way the King in this story loves the Shulamite is truly how the Lord feels about you. Just think of Jesus sitting next to you, tapping you on the shoulder, looking you in the eyes, and saying these words: "How beautiful you are. I am not disappointed with you—I am delighted in you."

"As I count the delights you bring to me. Love has become the greatest." This is the sacred journey! Jesus is enthralled, ravished, and passionate for His bride. Jesus is expressing the depths of the unconditional love filling His heart. Our love truly delights the holy heart of Jesus Christ. He enjoys our prayer life; He is thrilled each time He views us turning away from evil. The radiance of our faith, the contentment we find in Him—all of this enraptures the Son of God.

When we think of love's delights, we usually think of how it pleases our heart. But what pleasure floods Jesus Christ as we break our heart open to Him and give Him the treasures of our worship! How can we say our life is not significant if we understand that the purpose of life is to give Him pleasure? We really are one of the *"glorious ones fulfilling all His desires"* (Ps. 16:3)."[*] Jesus will have a bride who is pleasurable and utterly delightful to Him.

> **You stand in victory above the rest,**
> **stately and secure as you share with me your vineyard of love.**
> **Now I decree, I will ascend and arise.**
> **I will take hold of you with my power,**
> **possessing every part of my fruitful bride.**
> **Your love I will drink as wine,**
> **and your words will be mine. (7:7–8)**

"You stand in victory above the rest, stately and secure as you share with me your vineyard of love." Her stature speaks of her maturity, her character is *"stately and secure."* In most translations, her character is compared to the palm tree, which is a symbol of victory in the Scriptures.[**] The children waved palm branches at the victorious entry of Jesus into Jerusalem. We are given gifts and graces

---

[*] David knew that God delighted in him even while he was in fear and unbelief, stumbling in the city of Ziklag (Ps. 18:19).

[**] The palm stands upright with deep roots, so is the life of the victorious overcomer. The palm raises its beautiful crown to the heavens. It is described as one of the ornaments of Solomon's temple. See also Revelation 7:4.

of the Spirit to bring us into the stature of the fullness of Christ. She is bearing His image and growing into His fullness.

What victory surrounds her! Her life is upright, not twisted. She reaches for the heavens, knowing that is where her life is found (Col. 3:1–4). Her hidden life (roots) causes her to bear fruit and remain green and strong. All of her trials have only made her grow taller. She has the capacity to endure the dry seasons of life (Hab. 3:17–19). She now bears the life-giving fruit, the sweet fruits of spiritual maturity: discernment, gifting, anointing, and grace to feed others. Clusters of sweet fruit now adorn her life and the affections of her heart are full to bear blessing for others to enjoy.

"Now I decree, I will ascend and arise. I will take hold of you with my power, possessing every part of my fruitful bride." This is the declaration of the Bridegroom, that He will be united in power with the bride. In Acts 2, Jesus climbed the palm tree, which is a prophetic promise of end-time revival. The Son of God is ready to take over the church, filling its branches with His power and might. Jesus will once again ascend the tree of His planting. "Rise up, O Lord!" God has resolved to release revival power through the branches of this tree. Beloved, we are those branches. Jesus will lay hold of us in order to manifest His presence to the nations.

Signs and wonders are coming from the one who will take hold of us and make us His rod of might and wonder. Branch life will greatly increase in the coming days (Isa. 4:2). He will own the fruit as that which flows from Him, not something we produce in our own strength. This shows the strong desire of the King to apprehend the "palm tree bride." This verse is an incredible prophecy of what is to come:

Your love I will drink as wine, and your words will be mine. (7:8)

The Hebrew text is literally, "May the fragrance of your breath be like apples." Throughout the Song of Songs, the mouth speaks of intimacy with Jesus. The bride prayed in 1:2, *"Smother me with kisses—your Spirit-kiss divine. So kind are your caresses, I drink them in like the sweetest wine."* The Lord Jesus prophesies to the church that in the last days our intimacy with Him will be like the best wine. He has saved His best wine for last, and He freely shares it with His bride. The excellence of the Holy Spirit and the sweetest intimacy of the human spirit will pour out like wine through the end-time church. Our intimacy with Jesus is the best thing that the Spirit works in us for Jesus's sake.

We are to give the Lord the best we have in our relationship with Him. We must not neglect our intimacy with Him for any reason at all. Jesus said that the roof of the bride's mouth was the best wine of the Holy Spirit. The roof of the mouth refers to the palate of the mouth or the taste of her mouth, which means it is simply that which comes from her mouth. It is to be the best wine or that which brings the greatest joy to Jesus (4:10).

This is why Jesus turned water into wine at a wedding, thus teaching us of a greater wedding feast to come (John 2). We will grow to the place where we satisfy Him like nothing else, for He will empower us in this place of intimacy. Jesus calls intimacy with you the best wine of all. The most pleasurable thing outside of the Godhead is this love relationship between Christ and His bride.

The kiss of this passage is far different than the kiss of 1:2—this is *a kiss of restoration.* It is the kiss of the Father to his prodigal son who returned to his house (Luke 15:20). Here, the King is giving the Shulamite bride the depths of His redeeming love. He smells her breath and gives her a kiss to empower her. We need more than one kiss, however! We must be those who rely on the love of God (1 John 4:16).

"And your words will be mine." The revived church will nurture others with His words. All that He is will become ours as we give ourselves over to Him totally and completely. As we become one with Him, we release the power of the Spirit and impart sacred intimacy through the beautiful words of affirmation that we have

heard spoken over us. And those very same words that we have heard spoken over us, we will then speak over the brides-to-be, releasing an unstoppable power.

Pray this prayer today: "Lord Jesus, I want my words and my actions this day to make You known to others; I long to bring others into this sacred journey of finding every desire fulfilled in You. Make my life an advertisement of Your glory. Live Your life through me today, in Your holy name. Amen."

CHAPTER 32

HER DEEP FEELINGS OF LOVE

For your kisses of love are exhilarating,
more than any delight I've known before.
Your kisses of love awaken even the lips of sleeping ones
to kiss me as you have done. (7:9)

Jesus is interrupted by the maiden as she cannot hold it in any longer—she must tell Him how she feels at this time: *"For your kisses of love are exhilarating, more than any delight I've known before. Your kisses of love awaken even the lips of sleeping ones."* The wine of His love will revive those who are spiritually asleep, unaware that He is even near. It arouses our spirit until our lips move with praise and longing for Him.

The proof that the Spirit has awakened the sleepers is that their speech comes under His leadership. He will move the "sleepers" so that they speak in purity and righteousness. The Spirit will use the mature bridal partners of Jesus to awaken desire in the hearts of sleeping saints. Spirit-inspired speech will edify, challenge, exhort, and stir with passion the hearts of others.

The Holy Spirit flows gently in our hearts. Yes, He is like a river that is rushing, but the Spirit of God flows like wine, ever so gently and smoothly. The wine of the Spirit will go down smoothly because the bride receives it without resistance or without choking on it. To be continually filled with the Spirit means to continually live under the Holy Spirit's leadership (Eph. 5:18).

Now I know that I am filled with my beloved and all his desires are fulfilled in me. (7:10)

Behold the love of the Shulamite. Every other desire is lost in this love. She has become His Promised Land, His inheritance (Eph. 1:18). Her Lover owns her heart. He is all she cares about. Before now, fears and anxieties controlled her. All of life has now been given to Him alone.

It is a wonderful day when your identity becomes one that belongs to Him and not to yourself, your spouse, your family, or your church. We belong to the one who loved us out of sin and into salvation. This confession of our identity releases our inner man to love Him even more.

Our hearts break through the barrier of cold love when we speak these words: *"And all his desires are fulfilled in me."* As we go into the heart of Jesus, we gain insight into His affections toward us. The longings of His heart are really for us. Jesus lies awake at night thinking about His bride. The thoughts He has toward you are more than could be numbered (Ps. 139:17–18). He has engraved you on the palms of His hands (Isa. 49:16). How could He ever forget one who has been inscribed on His palm?

The desires and longings of the Son of God are toward you, even when you have forgotten about Him. His desire is ever toward you, never changing or shifting focus from you. Understanding this awakens an even deeper abandonment to Him. This is why we love Him, because He first loved us (1 John 4:19).

If we could really take this to heart, it would destroy depression's grip in our lives. To know that His desire is toward us would change our lives significantly. When we are accused wrongly and misunderstood, we can say, "His desire is for me." When we are criticized and slandered by others, we can say, "His desire is for me." Our source of emotional security is wrapped up in His statement of love over us. Our spirit jumps up and down inside when we hear it: "He really likes me!"

Our greatest glory is that we can move God's heart, which is deeply moved by our steady love for Him. The movements of our heart are so important to God that they are recorded in His books. The psalmist declared:

> You've kept track of all my wandering and my weeping.
> You've stored my many tears in your bottle—not one will be lost.
> You care about me every time I've cried.
> For it is all recorded in your book of remembrance (Ps. 56:8).

Do you know the way you move God? Weak people who truly love Him overcome Him. Our responsive love for Him is more precious than we understand. The bride did not know the impact her love was having on Jesus's heart because she did not feel His presence in the time of testing. Jesus reveals how He feels about our faithful love when we are in times of testing.

If God's desires are toward you, then no one can defeat you. Even your weaknesses will not turn you back when you can say, "His desire is for me." John, the beloved apostle, described himself as the "one Jesus loved." This was not to say that John was loved more, or to the exclusion of the other disciples, only that he identified himself in the love of God. Love taught him to say this. Can you say today, "I am the one Jesus loves"?

On the night Jesus was betrayed and beaten, He told His disciples of His desires for them. Knowing they would abandon Him and run, and knowing that they did not have enough strength to stand with Him in His hour of trial, His desire was still toward them. The affirmation of love comes to the weakest one, just like it comes to those who are faithful under pressure. Jesus's love for you is a torrent of passion that will not be turned aside because you fail Him. Nothing can separate you from His yearning love. It is impossible to be valued more than this.

Where is your focus today? Do your affections belong to your Lover, or have you spent them somewhere else? Do you see yourself alive on earth for His pleasure alone? Are you committed to whatever He desires? Let the fire of *His* desires tenderize your heart today. Hold your cold heart before the fire of His love until you can say, "I belong to my Lover and His desire is for me!"

Pray this prayer today: "I belong to You, Lord Jesus. All of Your desires are toward me, even when I am weak and confused. Come to me this day and sweep me away with You. I want my heart to burn with holy passion for You. I want my very life to be Your living sacrifice, pleasing and acceptable to You. Amen."

CHAPTER 33

COME AWAY

Come away, my lover.
Come with me to the far away fields.
We will run away together to the forgotten places
and show them redeeming love. (7:11)

The Shulamite's divine journey into the heart of Jesus is nearing an end. Grace has brought her safely thus far, and grace will lead her home; what tenderness she has discovered, what tender response she has given to Him. Everything He has told her is now bearing fruit. The one who stretched Himself out on the cross for her now stretches Himself out in fullness within her. She is learning to lean on Him; the two are becoming one.

This time, she will leave her comfort zone when He bids her come: *"Come away, my lover. Come with me to the far away fields."* Now she is ready to run with Him to the tops of the mountains and through every valley. The revelation He imparted in 7:5–9 has deeply changed her. A fresh commitment has been born to fulfill the Great Commission, touching the nations with His power. "Come," she cries out. His promise was, "I will come" (7:8). Therefore, as the awakened bride, she intercedes with the words, *"Come away, my Lover!"* His promises are meant to be fuel for intercessory fire.

The book is now coming to a full circle. In the beginning, the

King was drawing her, but now she is drawing Him. She is interceding for the villages and needy places of the earth to know this King. She was invited to join Him; now she invites Him to join her. *"Let us"* is used four times in 7:11–12. They are about to go forth in mature partnership, bringing the nations into the fiery love of the Father (Mark 16:20; 1 Cor. 15:10).

In the early days of her journey, the maiden was behind her wall, sitting on the couch, or at the banquet table, enjoying Him. He would come and ask her to follow Him. Each time, however, she refused. Convinced it would cost too much, her thoughts were, "But I might fail." Now, at the end of her journey, she is fearless. The dark trails no longer frighten her. She is willing to spend the night in faraway villages. As long as He is there, she has no fear of leaving the comfort zone. Her faith and obedience have grown—and so has yours.

The nature of a pilgrim is coming forth from within the Shulamite. Now she is content to go with Him from village to village, seeking lost and wounded sheep. Now she is content to be a stranger to this world's system, for she is truly free. Her confession is that of Ruth, "Wherever you go I will go, wherever you lodge, I will lodge. Your people are my people" (Ruth 1:16–17). The *countryside* speaks of the mission fields of the earth (Ps. 96:12–13; Prov. 31:16), and the *villages* represent local churches. She intercedes and asks for His manifest presence as they co-labor together.

The Hebrew word for *villages* may also be translated as "henna bushes." She pleads with Him to go and touch the world as they sleep among the henna bushes. Remember, the word for *henna* is the Hebrew word *kaphar,* meaning "to make atonement." The mature bride is willing to run to the ends of the earth to bring the message of love to those who have never heard.

The end-time bride will run with Jesus to those places where redemption is ready to be released to the people groups of the earth. This is the ministry of reconciliation the bride presents to the unbelieving world (2 Cor. 5:17–21). The two have become one, and the entire world will feel the impact of that union.

> **Let us arise and run to the vineyards of your people**
> **and see if the budding vines of love are now in full bloom.**
> **We will discover if their passion is awakened.**
> **There I will display my love for you. (7:12)**

The Shulamite is now thinking of others with compassion: *"Let us arise and run to the vineyards of your people."* No longer selfish, the Shulamite is longing to bless others she once disliked. Her desire is to see others succeed and blossom in the purpose of God. We must all realize that we are *all* important to Him. The heart of Jesus is thrilled over every local church, even those who have wounded us. Only the mature can run with Him in tenderness of heart to the villages of the body of Christ.

"Let us…see if the budding vines of love are now in bloom." At one time, the Bridegroom came to see if her vine was budding (6:11), but now they will go together to visit the needy and immature, to see their newly budding virtues. The anointing of Jesus causes the vine to bud. It was in the holy place that Aaron's rod burst forth with budding life when left overnight before God. When we go with Jesus, His presence causes life to spring forth.

I once had a dream where Billy Graham and I were together in a revival meeting where I was speaking. In the dream I had just preached to thousands—I was elated! But when I had finished ministering, Billy Graham placed his hand on my shoulder and looked deeply into my eyes, saying, "Don't be proud, Brian. Jesus Christ makes anyone look good!" Beloved, when we run with Jesus under His anointing, He makes anyone look good. All our fountains are found in Him.

Eagerness and zeal have energized the bride. She is willing to go and minister to others. Sacrifice is no longer avoided, for she will pay the price to touch others in His name. She will joyfully experience the urgency, the inconvenience, and the diligence of ministry. She is looking like Jesus as they co-labor in ministry. His kingdom business is her first priority. She labors not merely for herself, but for others. How deeply the cross has dealt with her!

The budding vines speak of the churches and ministries that are immature, not fully developed in the ways of divine grace. She has love to share, fruit to impart, and gifts to empower. Eager to present others *"perfect in Christ"* (Col. 1:28), her cry is to bless them—freely she has received and now freely she will give. Her heart is turned toward cultivating the garden of God in others. This is apostolic grace equipping her for ministry.

At first, she lamented that others had made her a keeper of the vineyard, wearying her with their work. Now she joyfully serves others in the vineyards out in the countryside. Because the Shulamite loves Him, she is feeding His lambs (John 21:15–17). During her immature years, serving others became a distraction from her enjoyment of Him. Ministry was a hindrance. But now, in full union with Him, she has become a vessel possessed by His life. Ministry cannot distract her or separate her from His presence. She is His chariot of fire.

We will discover if their passion is awakened.
There I will display my love for you. (7:12)

"There," in the place of giving her life for others, in the place of sacrificial service among the immature budding vines, is where she risks persecution and injury. Away from her comfort zone, out in the countryside, *there* she gives Him her undistracted love and affection, even in the midst of labor, toil, pain, and disappointment in ministry. Surrounded by spiritual warfare and conflicts, with fears within and pressures around her, yet she can say, *"There I will display my love for you."* The Father will prepare a bride for Jesus who will not only love Him in a cozy church or in isolation from the tensions of life, but a bride who loves Him in the hardest of times, in the hardest of places.

Some have translated this verse, "There I will give you my

caresses." Can you give Him the sweetness of love in the midst of the battle? It is one thing to love Jesus in a cave, but it is only mature love that can keep our eyes on Him on the battlefield. True apostolic Christianity is coming. It will be seen in sacred intimacy, sacrificial ministry, and faithfulness in suffering (Phil. 3:10).

Nothing can diminish our love for Him when we are consumed with holy passion for Jesus. The hassles of ministry with the immature, the pressures and hardships of life, nothing will intimidate the victorious bride. She is running with Him in bridal partnership. Are you there yet? Are you running with the Son of God as He blesses the nations with His love?

> **The love apples are in bloom,**
> **sending forth their fragrance of spring.**
> **The rarest of fruits are found at our doors—**
> **the new as well as the old.**
> **I have stored them for you, my lover-friend! (7:13)**

The bride is longing for love. Mandrakes were known as "love apples." They come from a small tree that yields little round aromatic apples. Purple in color and with a beautiful fragrance, they speak of royal love. They were believed to be an aid in bearing children, facilitating wedded love (Gen. 30:14–16).

Mandrakes bloom during wheat harvest. The bride is working with the King to bring in the great harvest of souls. As she smells the mandrakes nearby, it reminds her again of the tender love He has shown to her. She is not content to be just the bride; she wants to become the mother of the King's child.

The Shulamite is seeking for a Son to be born in her. This is the longing of the church in these closing days of human history, to have Christ formed in us (Gal. 4:19). This loving partnership will bear fruit. There will come a corporate expression of Christ on earth through the bride that is in union with Jesus. This many-membered body will be seen in the lives of a people who have died to self and are alive to God. Robed with the sun, the moon under her feet, and a crown with twelve stars on her head, the bride will be with child (Rev. 12:1–2)!

"The rarest of fruits are found at our doors." Their honeymoon house is nearby. As they enter, every delicacy imaginable is present. Love is in the air. Their glad experiences are shared as they labor together in the harvest. These are the pleasant fruits of a shared life, as the two partake together of grace and glory. Like delicacies to the soul are the fruits of yielding to His life within. In Him she now lives, in Him she now moves, and in Him she has her being.

"The new as well as the old. I have stored them for you, my Lover-Friend!" She draws from deep experiences of the past and the ever-fresh revelation of today. O, the joys they share in partnership together. She does not come in from the harvest field empty-handed (1 Thess. 2:19–20). These are the firstfruits of the harvest, her wave offering! New experiences of mercy flow from the treasure house of holy love. Continuous harvest reaps continuous happiness (Lev. 26:10). Her treasures are stored up in heaven to be cast at His feet as her eternal love offering.

We have new fruits, new joys to offer to our King. We have new places in our hearts that we have never yet surrendered, and new prayers that we've never yet offered to Him. But we have some old fruits too. There is the choice fruit of our first love, and Jesus delights in it. We have old testimonies of God's faithfulness to us to keep His promises. Offer to Him today both old and new.

Pray this prayer today: "I give You, Lord Jesus, the praise of my lips and the offering of my life. Everything I am is because of Your kindness and love. Thank You, Jesus, for every kiss and embrace You have showered upon me. I am blessed, filled, and encouraged today, just thinking of You. Help me to live each moment in the conscious awareness of Your love. Amen."

CHAPTER 34

HER LOVE GROWS BOLD

**If only I could show everyone
this passionate desire I have for you.
If only I could express it fully,
no matter who was watching me,
without shame or embarrassment. (8:1)**

L ooking Him in the eyes, she opens her heart to share a secret
with Him. She is concerned about her public display of
affection. This was improper for her culture and her people. Public kissing was a violation of the standards of decency.
The only exceptions to this were between blood relatives, such as
between a brother and a sister. However, the Shulamite longs to
boldly show her loyalty and love to such a marvelous King as this.
If only He were a brother, she could be affectionate in public with
no embarrassment whatsoever. But He is her Lover.

The bride longs for a full manifestation of their oneness in
their relationship. She cannot hide her love for such a King. At
the first, she would cry out for His kiss, but now she would find
and actually kiss Him. Others do not understand the passion of
the church for one like Jesus. They mistake our abandonment to
Him as foolishness. Even within the church, it is those who are

most visible and outward in their affection for Jesus who bring up a religious spirit in the proud of heart. To see someone lavish his or her love on Jesus in a public worship service is disgusting to the self-righteous. The bride prays for boldness to overcome the fear of what others think.

> **I long to bring you to my innermost chamber—**
> **this holy sanctuary you have formed within me.**
> **O that I might carry you within me.**
> **I would give you the spiced wine of my love,**
> **this full cup of bliss that we share.**
> **We would drink our fill until... (8:2)**

We usually think of the King leading us. How bold. We truly can bring Him to others through prevailing prayer and holy love. She longs to bring His presence into the church, her mother's house (Gal. 4:26). His anointing is what they need, and she knows it.

Jesus will actually let you lead Him. He gives you kingdom authority and He cooperates with your decisions. Only the mature will discover the fullness of this partnership of grace. As an usher would lead one to the front row, the place of honor, so the bride desires to bring Jesus into the church and usher Him into the highest place. Not content to kiss Him in public, she wants to bring Him back to the people who first taught her. She remembers those who have taught her and blessed her in the past, and now she brings home the blessing of passionate love for Jesus.

The bride promises to serve the Bridegroom the wine of her love. Wine mixed with spices is more expensive and more enjoyable; she will give Him her very best and costly adoration. She has become His very own cup of delight. We have the wonderful privilege of worshiping Jesus Christ. We have something sweet to offer Him each time our hearts open in praise. Our emotions are stirred, as they should be. Our hearts break open with perfumed praises. Sitting at His feet, we discover a union with the Son of God. This is how life is meant to be!

> **His left hand cradles my head**
> **while his right hand holds me close.**
> **We are at rest in this love. (8:3)**

He places His left hand under her head, upholding her thoughts that she might rest in the assurance of His love. *"While his right hand holds me close"*—the displays of power with the right hand and the hidden demonstrations of care with the left hand hold her tight. *"We are at rest in this love"*—the full embrace of His love has come. He is able to love her completely and embrace her for life in His loving arms. She no longer doubts His care, for He has come in answer to her prayer. This embrace is what sustains the church. He holds us near to His heart when days of darkness surround the bride. Have you hugged your Lord today? The arms that moved to shape a universe will move at the sound of your cry and hold you near.

> **Promise me, brides-to-be, by the gentle gazelles and delicate deer,**
> **that you'll not disturb my love until she is ready to arise. (8:4)**

Holding her like this, the King turns to the daughters of Jerusalem as they stand nearby, and says to them, *"Promise me, brides-to-be, by the gentle gazelles and delicate deer, that you'll not disturb my love until she is ready to arise."* Jesus will speak with authority to those who may misunderstand our love-embrace with the Bridegroom.

We must leave this "charge" to Him. He is exhorting the maidens to refrain from disturbing her in this divine moment of glory with the King. He has spoken these words three times in the song. Her days of fear and timidity are over, and she is caught up with Him, not with how it looks to others. Jesus will guard her in His grace until His purpose for her comes to pass and the full power of His glory rises up within her in power, *"until she is ready to arise."*

The Bridegroom-King says:

Who is this one? Look at her now!
She arises out of her desert, clinging to her beloved.
When I awakened you under the apple tree,
as you were feasting upon me,
I awakened your innermost being with the travail of birth
as you longed for more of me. (8:5)

The voice of the Holy Spirit is heard as He prophesies of the victorious church: *"Who is this? Look at her now! She arises out of her desert."* The Shulamite is seen coming up from the wilderness leaning on her Beloved. Who is this who has persevered through the wilderness testing, the lonely difficulties of life? There is nothing like the bride in all of human history. She is a company of passionate people who have one goal for their existence, to be one with the Son of God. She has passed the tests of life. She has journeyed through the dark nights and hard trials. She is His overcoming bride.

She is ascending out of the wilderness, *"clinging to her Beloved."* She did not quit but remained faithful. Love kept her heart faithful to the Bridegroom. Anybody can quit in the wilderness—only the one in love will stay true. Sometimes we have wanted to quit, but our love for Him kept us loyal. She will come up out of the wilderness no matter what, for she loves Him. The religious motivation of guilt, shame, and fear are not sufficient; love is. Her walk is ascension of the hidden stairway. Like the vision Jacob saw at Bethel, the Jesus stairway is before her.

The Shulamite has walked up out of the desert into His end-time glory. She had been unable to leave the wilderness of spiritual wandering until she clung to Him. Purified by fire, she is a bride making herself ready for the eternal city. The Holy Spirit is prophesying her ultimate triumph by the power of God. Before Jesus was born, the Father promised the Son a loyal bride, one who would cling to Him. The Father arranged a marriage before the world was formed. You, beloved, are part of that loving company of virgins with one holy desire—to be one with Him.

"Clinging to her Beloved." This is where we are meant to be. With a loyal love, her heart rests securely on His breast (John 13:23). He is her life source, her supply, her strength, her comfort, and her lover. God's desires for you will come to pass just as they have for the maiden. This prophetic declaration is to be sung as a love song over you.

The day will come when all that is within you will be lost in Him forever. Song of Songs 8:5 is your destiny. The Lord's strategy throughout your life has been to produce in you an attitude of total dependency on Him (Jer. 9:23). Loving hearts will find no confidence in self but will discover an endless source of life in Him (2 Cor. 3:5–6). As we mesh our hearts with His, we absorb His life. It bleeds through. We begin to flow in His wisdom, not in our cleverness. We touch His power, not our feeble strivings. We are allowed to tap into unfailing love instead of our love with strings attached. We must keep leaning harder and harder into Him until it is asked with amazement, "Who is this, clinging to his or her Lover?" Notice the different ways we cling or depend on Him:

- *To be saved from sin.* We must cling to the cross of our Beloved and find His blood as the only antidote for sin's guilt.
- *To live above the power of sin.* We must cling to His life within us to conquer sin's power. Determination, discipline, prayer, and godly friends all contribute, but only His indestructible life released in us can deliver us from sin. We cling to Him for our victory. We are weak and insufficient, but He is mighty and able to rescue.
- *To walk in emotional wholeness.* We cling to Him to be free from the wounds of our past and the difficulties

of our environment. He was bruised, rejected, and despised, yet He lived the most whole and balanced life. This will be released in our emotional makeup as we lean on our Lover. All the self-protecting "mechanisms" are abandoned when we lean on Him.

- *To receive guidance and direction for our lives.* Clinging to the Lord Jesus for wisdom will be the only sure way of discerning the will of God. He has the power to turn our hearts toward Him, causing us to *want* the will of God. He has the power to intervene in our circumstances, making them line up correctly with His purposes.

- *To be provided for and loved.* Jesus alone must be our source of supply. He is in our midst as one who serves. Dwelling within us, He "serves" us with every needed virtue. As we cling to Him we will have no lack. All good things come from Him who loved us and gave Himself for us (Isa. 41:17–20).

Our lives have been spent not leaning on our own understanding or on our own clever ability to find a way out of every mess we get into. Often, the last thing we do is look to Him. We have been taught to stand on our own, to become our own savior. We wander from Him rather than cling to Him. But all of this is about to change. The prophecy of the Holy Spirit has now been sung over us—we *will* come up out of our desert clinging to our Beloved.

When you see Him as your Beloved, you will want to cling to Him. The Lord has used the desert to break you; it has served its purpose. Like Jacob leaning on his staff, you must cling to and lean on the Lord as you walk forward. Unable to plan your own way, He is becoming the light unto your path. The stubborn heart of stone has been replaced with a heart of flesh that responds to His gaze (Ezek. 36:26–27; Ps. 32:8; Prov. 1:23).

As a poor sinner, the Shulamite was sought by the Lord,

discovered beneath the apple tree and loved just as she was: *"When I awakened you under the apple tree, as you were feasting upon me, I awakened your innermost being."* The apple tree is a picture of Christ in the fullness of His love. Under the shadow of His eternal love, her Beloved awakened her to see the cross.

If Jesus had not stirred your heart and roused you to seek Him, then you would be lost. We owe it all to Him. It was the sovereign work of the Spirit of God that initiated our salvation and all spiritual progress in our lives. He comes to knock on the doors of our hearts to rouse us in holy passion for Jesus. God is the author of our natural and spiritual birth.

The Lord is pleased to use us to awaken the hearts of others and confront them with their need for salvation. All of us heard the gospel from someone else, and we become part of God's way of awakening sinners to Christ. God is our Father and the church is like our mother. The church labors *"with the travail of birth"* through intercession and the preaching of the gospel, giving birth to converts (Rev. 12:2). And she is motivated by her intense longing to see more of Christ birthed in the earth. These converts then become the daughters of Jerusalem until they are captured by holy affections and begin their own glorious Shulamite journey.

Pray this prayer today: "Lord Jesus, I long to be a cup of bliss for You to drink. I yearn to be Your loyal loving friend, always at Your side and always satisfying Your heart. Receive my worship and my love, King of Glory. Thank You for making me one with You! Amen."

CHAPTER 35

THE FIERY SEAL OF LOVE

Fasten me upon your heart as a seal of fire forevermore.
This living, consuming flame
will seal you as my prisoner of love.
My love is stronger than the chains of death and the grave,
all consuming as the very flashes of fire
from the burning heart of God.
Place this fierce, unrelenting fire over your entire being. (8:6)

This is the wonderful invitation of Jesus to the mature bride: *"Fasten me upon your heart."* Her journey began with a longing for kisses and ends with the fiery seal of divine love encasing her heart. He was the one who awakened her, and He will be the one to preserve her blameless in His love.

This seal is for protection, preservation, and passion, a seal of promise, approval, and favor. It is also a seal of ownership, for she belongs to the King. It is a royal seal that cannot be broken (breaking a royal seal meant certain death in the days of Solomon). This is not a seal made of wax, but a supernatural seal made of love. It is the power of supernatural love released in her heart by the Holy Spirit. Jesus invites her to place Him as that seal of love throughout her days.

"As a seal of fire forevermore." As the Lord Jesus becomes the fiery seal over our hearts, we are progressively brought into the ownership of Jesus Christ. He possesses our soul, our feelings, our spirit, and our life. Divine love is the seal, not our past victories or discipline over the flesh. It is not our devotion to Him that seals us, nor is it our past failures—it is Him alone.

The Hebrew word for *seal* can also be translated "a prison cell." The Lord Jesus wants to imprison us in His love. What a blessed prison is the seal of His love! Perhaps this is what Paul the apostle recognized in calling himself *"the prisoner of the Lord"* (Eph. 4:1). In the prison cell of His love, we discover that only His will and pleasure is our delight. Satisfaction comes when we abandon our small goals for becoming one with Him.

How do we place Jesus as a fiery seal of love over our hearts? It is simply by communing with Him. As we place our hearts before Him, we take Him inside of us through divine fellowship and He covers our hearts with a wedding canopy of love. Scripture also says that *"this living, consuming flame will seal you as my prisoner of love,"* thus sealing us from our foes and locking us into Him. He carries us moment by moment over His heart—now we must set Him our as a love seal over ours.

Some translations also add, "Like a seal on your arm." The heart is the place of love and the arm is where strength resides. Jesus wants to be a fiery seal over our affections and our strength. What we need the most, Jesus will supply—passion and power. Jesus Himself will seal our arms with divine anointing and strength. We are enabled by His borrowed life to minister to others. The anointing is our secret strength. With sealed arms, we can impart blessings and holy passion to others. And as we minister with Jesus as the seal on our arms, we are preserved from "burnout" in ministry. Spiritual buoyancy characterizes our ministries when our arms are sealed in omnipotent love. Supernatural grace just flows from the seal upon our arms.

Our service is sanctified when Jesus is our secret source of strength. We mount up with eagle's wings and run without weariness. The busy activities of the flesh only leave us exhausted, as we make futile efforts to do it all. In His strength, with our arms sealed in fiery love, every act of service flows from a more pure fountain. This twofold bridal seal on our arms and on our hearts will be the joy of life. We can endure anything when our emotions and our strength flow out from His love.

"My love is stronger than the chains of death and the grave." How strong are death and the grave? There is no one who escapes their grasp. Death is the king of terrors. All the tears and sorrow, and the sighs of loved ones, nothing can free one who is held in their grip. Human power is hopeless in the face of death. Who can escape its stronghold over this fallen world? You cannot bribe death with money nor persuade it to go away. Death watches over its victims and holds them in an unshakable vise. Nobody escapes the grave. Death is a prevailing, comprehensive power. Once it holds you, it will not let you go.

Yet this is what God's love is like. God's love holds you fast and will never let you go. You may run from His love, but it will seek you out. Relentless, omnipotent love will eventually win. There is a power to the love of Jesus that claims everything. He is not content with a partial ownership of our hearts. His is a jealous love. Jesus walked in that love toward the Father; zeal for His Father's house consumed Him (John 2:17). The jealousy of His love is pure, a manifestation of intense longing to have us as His Promised Land (James 4:5; Eph. 1:18). It is His fiery envy to make us pure for the Son of God.

What could be crueler than the grave? It is unmoved by the tears of others when we lower our loved ones into the dark tomb of death. The grave knows no pity, no sympathy. Just as the grave will not let go of its victims, so Jesus's love will not surrender you or ever let you go. You were meant for Him. Your journey is into His fiery, jealous heart of love. Never will He let you go. How intense is His love for weak, still struggling believers!

Jesus is about to release a love to His bride that is so comprehensive, so jealous, that it can only be compared to death and the grave. It will capture us in our failures and heal us completely. Never resting until we are perfected in grace, this love will operate through every pain and pleasure of life until we are like the Lord Jesus. The Father loved His Son so much that He decided to populate heaven with people just like Him. You might as well surrender now, for His love will win in the end.

When Jesus gave Himself for us on the cross, He was thinking of you and me. He was looking to the time when you would take Him as a seal upon your heart. For Him, the grave was not cruel; it was the means to find you. The last words of our Lord Jesus as He offered Himself to God were, "It is finished." Completed. Done. In the Aramaic language, the language of Jesus, the word He actually spoke was *kalah*, which has two meanings: it means to be "finished or accomplished," and to be a "bride." The very last word of your King as He died for you was a sigh for His bride. He died for His bride!

Jesus's inflamed desire for you is beyond knowledge or analysis. He drinks of your love, feasts on your adoration, and He is moved powerfully by your worship. Though He lacks nothing, you complete Him. Not needing a thing, yet He longs for more of you. The splendor of God is that Jesus finds delight in the immature and incomplete ones, watching with ecstatic joy as you grow up into the image of Christ. One day everything you love about Jesus will be said of you. You'll look just like the one you adore.

"All consuming as the very flashes of fire from the burning heart of God." The flashes of love that come from the heart of Jesus are like solar flares. The blazing fire of the Son of God will consume us in the end. We will be captured and ruined by His love. In the prison cell of love, fire surrounds us; its bolts are bolts of fire, furious flames enflaming the human heart. The very lightning of God will envelop our souls as He becomes the bridal seal that is set upon us. What kind of love is this? What kind of burning fire

is His love? It burns like the flame of Jehovah, the burning fires of Almighty God. To touch love is to touch God, for our God is a consuming fire.

The phrase *"the very flashes of fire from the burning heart of God"* can also be translated here as "a most vehement flame." It is actually two Hebrew words: the first means "a flash of fire" or "sharply polished point of a weapon," and the second word in the phrase is "Yah," which is the sacred name of God Himself! Add the two words together *(shalhebet-yaah)* and you get, "The Lord most vehement or passionate."

This mighty flame is nothing less than the very flame of Jehovah. It is a supernatural burning of God in the soul (Luke 24:32; Isa. 4:4). One of the first revelations of God given in the Scripture is Deuteronomy 4:24 (NIV), *"Our God is a consuming fire."* He defines Himself as one with a hot, passionate love for His people that will consume and destroy every distraction from holiness.

God has fiery emotions that burn in His heart. He is a passionate God who will baptize His bride in the consuming ocean of His eternal love. When we think of God's fire, we often think of judgment. But God's fire is first a fire of passion for His people. Jesus looks with eyes of fire upon His bride (Rev. 19:12). This is not a fire of judgment, but a passionate, fiery gaze meant to consume us.

"Place this fierce, unrelenting fire over your entire being." Undistracted devotion to Jesus will brand the heart with burning passions. Nothing can be compared to this love. Intense, unyielding, like a million nuclear reactors of blazing fire. This is the seal He invites you to place over your heart. It is a seal that will brand you for life, forever changing you by that love. It will consume your shackles and chains of emotional bondage and pain; it will unravel your clever ways and break the self-confidence that has been a part of your life.

When a love like this gets ahold of you, it is like the eruption of a holy volcano within you. The lava of His love will scorch your flesh life, burning up the dross of earthly ambition and pride. It is an unquenchable fire that will not rest until you are fully His. Regardless of your sin or failure, this relentless love that consumes like a forest fire will defeat it. It is a tenderizing fire that will leave you responsive to Him, craving more. You are about to become His burning bush of fire (Exod. 3:2).

Rivers of pain and persecution will never extinguish this flame.
Endless floods will be unable
to quench this raging fire that burns within you.
Everything will be consumed.
It will stop at nothing
as you yield everything to this furious fire
until it won't even seem to you like a sacrifice anymore. (8:7)

These waters are floods of obstacles and pressures. Nothing can put out the eternal flame of divine love that is burning within the bride. Water puts out fire, but many waters cannot quench this love! Even rivers of persecution cannot do it. Rivers of misunderstanding, heartache, disappointment, or pain cannot quench His love. Likewise, neither can rivers of accusation, condemnation, and rejection put out the sacred flame. Joseph felt temptation, Peter denied our Lord Jesus, Saul of Tarsus persecuted the saints—but nothing could extinguish love's jealous flames for them.

This supernatural fire fell from heaven, consuming the living sacrifices of the bridal company. It will not go out. Sickness, failure, divorce, shame, and guilt—none of these can quench the love of God. Jesus will never put out the fire that burns in our hearts. We can be fired from our job, kicked out of our church, and rejected by those we love—but the strongest rivers of difficulty cannot put out this blazing fire that still burns within (Rev. 12:16–17).

His love is the seal, and the source of this love is God Himself. Our ability to claim this love has nothing to do with our temperament or our personality, how we have treated Him or what we have done to mess up our lives. His love is the seal over our hearts—not our performance and not our devotion. His fire is greater than the illegal fires of sexual sin, pornography, or drug addiction. His fire will not be put out by your failure to walk perfectly before Him. His love is the seal, not your secret failures and shameful history. This love will prevail, for it will conquer you in the end—you will be consumed in its flames. Love conquers all and never fails (1 Cor. 13:8–13). When you fail, love doesn't. Your life, your home, your wealth, and your ministry are nothing compared to this priceless love. You would gladly give it all away to know a love like this!

"Everything will be consumed. It will stop at nothing as you yield everything to this furious fire until it won't even seem to you like a sacrifice anymore." This speaks of a man who would sacrificially give up everything he has to help the one he truly loves. This is a wholehearted love for Jesus. He is everything to the one who loves Him: *"It won't even seem to you like a sacrifice anymore."* This is the first commandment being fulfilled in a human life—to love God with all of our heart, all of our mind, and all of our strength. This is where the kisses of 1:2 will take us.

When you are in love with someone, you don't worry about the cost involved in lavishing love on that person. A man will spend thousands of dollars on an engagement ring for the one he loves without a second thought. He has a love without price tags. A person in love does not worry about sacrifice—there is no limit to what he or she will give. To call it a sacrifice is an insult.

Imagine having a child who could only be spared from death if you would sell your home or car, and spend your life savings—everything you had—to pay for the treatment that could save her life. Would you do it? Yes, if you love her you would. You would utterly scorn the "things" of this life in order to have the one thing that matters most—the life of your daughter. And you would not even consider it a sacrifice. It is all nothing compared to the life of your loved one. Love will prompt you to lay it all aside without regard to cost. This is the love that will abide in the bride as she is presented to Jesus on His wedding day.

Love motivated Paul to write in Philippians 3:8, *"To truly know him meant letting go of everything from my past and throwing all my boasting and all that I thought made me better than others on the garbage heap. It's all like a pile of manure to me now, so that I may be enriched in the reality of knowing Jesus Christ and embrace him as Lord in all of his greatness."* When love sacrifices, there is no loss involved. Put everything in life on one side of a scale, and then put knowing Jesus on the other side—which would be the side to win your heart? When we taste the indescribable delight of knowing the Son of God, when we see His beauty and drink the wine of His love, we can live for nothing else.

If all the wealth of the world were to be given to you if you would deny Him, you would love Him still. If the entire honor in the world were to be laid at your feet if you would deny Him, you would love Him still. Jesus is the reward of love. He is enough for every captured heart. Ask the Lord to come upon your heart as a fiery seal. Ask Him to energize all your labors for Him as the secret source of strength. Ask Him to give you that sacred flame, burning with all its intensity until it consumes you. Ask Him to release a grace to love Him with all your heart, mind, and strength, until the shadows flee and the night gives way to His brilliant day.

Pray this prayer today: "Jesus, I want more grace to love You more. Strengthen my heart until a greater love flows to You. I want to love You with all my heart, all my mind, and all my strength. Send Your light and truth into my heart this day. Amen."

CHAPTER 36

THE BRIDE INTERCEDES

My brothers said to me when I was young,
"Our sister is so immature.
What will we do to guard her for her wedding day?" (8:8)

T he bride remembers how her brothers helped her mature and grow in her love for Christ. Now she longs to help others in much the same way. The spiritually strong and mature are always ready and willing to help the weak. Immature believers are under the responsibility of the bride. The Shulamite turns to look upon the other maidens and begins to intercede for others in the body. With the seal of bridal love on her heart, she grows in her concern for those who have yet to make the journey. There are still those who are immature in Christ and who do not know the depths of His love; they have yet to hear the "cooing of doves."

We must pray as the Shulamite did and give ourselves to the young sisters and brothers. Our life vision must include preparing others to be part of the marvelous company called the virgin bride of Christ (2 Cor. 11:2). The bride understands now that she has a responsibility to bless the young, immature ones in Christ. She is willing to partner with Jesus in laboring among the young sisters (Matt. 12:50). They have not yet cried out for the kisses and for the drawing of His heart; she will be the one to pray and show them the way. The maiden must help them grow in the courage and confidence that He loves them in the midst of their weaknesses. The bride has a deep sense of responsibility for immature believers (6:11; 7:11). This is the heart of a spiritual father (1 Thess. 2:11). She is not content to go on in the Lord without helping others wholeheartedly follow Jesus.

Many in the church today are unable to be a source of encouragement and care for others, as they need constant care themselves. Overwhelmed with their own problems, they have yet to develop and mature so they are able to richly bless others in the body of Christ. Lacking character, patience, wisdom, and discernment, they are as yet unprepared for servant ministry in the church.

"What will we do to guard her for her wedding day?" The wedding day for this young sister is coming and she is still unprepared. The Lord is about to come to this young sister and take her hand in marriage. Her courtship is about to begin. Our intercession prepares the way for ministry to touch and equip her with a passion to wholeheartedly pursue Jesus. In the day of God's visitation, He will require a measure of maturity from the "young" ones (Eph. 4:13). This is now the engagement time, but the wedding is at hand. We must labor to present a mature body to Jesus on that day (Col. 1:28–29).

The Bridegroom-King says:

"We will build a tower of redemption to protect her.
Since she is vulnerable,
we will enclose her with a wall of cedar boards." (8:9)

The Shulamite will look upon others and seek to help them in their sacred journey. He says, *"Since she is vulnerable, we will enclose her with a wall of cedar boards."* Cities with walls were well defended, while cities without walls were vulnerable to the attack of their foes.[*] "Wall ministries" either function in a pastoral way

---

[*] See Jer. 1:18–19.

to protect the people from the enemy or they raise up God's prophetic standard, thus establishing God's line of demarcation for holiness in the land.

In Song of Songs 8:10, the bride speaks of herself as a wall ministry. This involves protecting others and being a prophetic standard bearer. There are pressures associated with being a wall. When the enemy shoots arrows, the wall stands in the path of the arrows meant for the young ones. This is a picture of taking her forward in her spiritual battles, helping her in the fight of faith and keeping her well protected. With their help she will be able to see where the enemy is coming at her and use the weapons of redemption to defend herself (Ps. 127:1).

This impartation of supernatural grace is meant to guard her from harm. With apostolic maturity, the Shulamite is ready to build towers in the lives of others. These towers will strengthen them in the Lord. The bride says to Jesus, "We will build her a battlement." The battlement, or tower, of a fortress was on the top where the archers shot through the indentations in the stone. They shot and then stood behind the stone battlements for protection. The battlements provided places for the watchmen to spot and shoot the enemy and thus defend the city.

"We will enclose her with a wall of cedar boards." The cedar boards are expensive, strong, and fragrantly scented. Cedars often speak of humanity. Boards of cedar enclosing the Shulamite's life speak of the fragrance of the life of Jesus surrounding her labors. The cedars in the temple were overlaid with gold (1 Kings 6:20–22). And Jesus is the fragrant cedar of Lebanon (3:9). Enclosed in Him, clothed with Jesus Christ, the bride will go on to touch many for the gospel. This is being clothed with Jesus Christ.

Some ministries in the body function as walls to protect and bless others. They are discerning the times accurately and are able to give much to others. Pastors and prophets are often like walls that give definition and care to local churches. Some ministries are like doors to new things. They are teachers and evangelists who open doors to evangelism and new truths. Some protect, some open doors—we need them both. But all must be passionate flames of fire for Jesus.

Again, notice what the King declares: *"We will build towers... we will enclose her."* He will not carry out His purposes of grace without using the bride. She will be His partner, His helpmeet, His hands. They are one in love and one in labor. The sweetness of their union is now complete.

What a picture we have here. The King is jubilant, the bride is radiant, the Son is magnificent, the daughters are joyous, and the young sister is resplendent with shining silver and fragrant with cedar. The work of redeeming grace is manifesting in the church. This holy family will shine forth, casting out darkness from the created order. The kingdom is coming. The bride has a place at His side that no other may have. She is His queen, His coruler over all things. She has made herself ready to sit with Him on the throne. She will bring forth the "spiritual seed" that will crush the head of the serpent, as the Lamb's wife dwells with Him forever.

Pray this prayer today: "Help me, Lord Jesus, to care for others. I need to love them, serve them, and show them Your great love. Let me take every opportunity that comes to me today to demonstrate kindness and mercy to all. Amen."

CHAPTER 37

THE HAPPIEST OF ENDINGS

But now I have grown and become a bride,
and my love for him has made me
a tower of passion and contentment for my beloved.
I am now a firm wall of protection for others,
guarding them from harm.
This is how he sees me—I am the one who brings him bliss,
finding favor in his eyes. (8:10)

What a sacred journey this has been. It's the mystical, mysterious journey of our soul into the heart of Jesus Christ. This is the great Song of Songs that will endure throughout eternity as the song of the Lamb (Rev. 15:3–4).

The Shulamite's final declaration in the song is a revelation of what she has become in His eyes: *"But now I have grown and become a bride and my love for him has made me a tower of passion and contentment for my Beloved."* Is this how you see yourself? Your Lover-King has made you into one who satisfies. The seal of fiery love has transformed you from a nobody into a beautiful partner.

Towers are seen from great distances, which means the bride has a trans-local sphere of ministry (Isa. 54:11–17). Now she has become one who has grown to a place of maturity, bringing great contentment to Jesus. His heart has longed for His flock to be cared for and protected. The Shulamite has become a shepherd after His own heart.

As the Shulamite gives herself for others, the heart of Jesus is content and satisfied with her life. Her destiny is being fulfilled— she has found peace in His eyes. Like Mary, the mother of Jesus, she has found great favor with God. She is a wall, a tower, and one who brings contentment and peace to the heart of the King of Kings. A remarkable confidence now fills her heart as she is ready to be forever His.

"I am now a firm wall of protection for others, guarding them from harm." As a wall, the stones and arrows would hit her before they could harm others. She stands mature and faithful in the day of battle. How the church needs mature ones like her in our own day! She commits herself to enclose and protect the local churches (cities). She leads by example and stands firm on behalf of others. It's time for you to say:

I am the one who brings him bliss,
finding favor in his eyes.
My bridegroom-king has a vineyard of love
made from a multitude of followers.
His caretakers of this vineyard
have given my beloved their best. (8:11)

This short parable (8:11–12) speaks of the accountability of the Lord's people. He will entrust us with stewardship in His vineyard and reward us accordingly. Every lover of God will one day stand before the judgment seat of Christ to receive reward or suffer loss (1 Cor. 3:11–15; 2 Cor. 5:10; Rom. 14:12–14).

The figure of a vineyard is seen frequently in Scripture as

the work of feeding, leading, and maturing God's people (Isa. 5; Matt. 25; John 15). The Lord of the vineyard will one day return and demand an accounting for what has been lent to us.*

"My Bridegroom-King has a vineyard of love made from a multitude of followers." In my research I found that the vineyard referred to here is the vineyard of Baal. This speaks of the church of Jesus Christ that reaches throughout all the earth. The Hebrew text literally says, "Solomon had a vineyard at Baal-Hamon."

The king's vineyard is a picture of the church, the called-out multitude of those who follow Jesus. Baal-Hamon can be also be translated "lord of a multitude," "lord of an uproar," or "lord of wealth." Jesus is the master of many servants, each one different and vital. Before the Lord returns, we expect a great harvest from among the nations, a multitude of souls redeemed by His fiery love (Rev. 14:14–16). Jesus will be seen as the "Lord of a multitude" of lovers who will follow Him anywhere.

"His caretakers of this vineyard have given my Beloved their best." Solomon leased his vineyard to tenants, or keepers (Matt. 21:33). Likewise, Jesus has given us the responsibility to keep His flock, tend His vines, and bring forth fruits of righteousness (1 Cor. 3:9; Mark 16:20). Jesus is the rightful owner of the kingdom of God and may give the responsibilities of the kingdom to whomsoever He wishes to tend. The caretakers of the Lord's vineyard will have the privilege and reward of bringing to Him the abundance of fruit from the maturing lives of those they shepherd. Precious fruit will come forth and be gathered to the Lord from the multitudes.

As God gives the increase, the faithful labors of many will bear fruit. The Hebrew for *"their best"* is literally "a thousand shekels of silver," representing the fullness of maturity that will spring forth from their labors. Isaiah 7:23 supplies an excellent commentary on this truth: *"In that day, in every place where there were a thousand*

---

* The vineyard the Shulamite kept in chapter 1 was the King's vineyard. These "tenants" were the very ones who offended the maiden in the beginning, but now she understands more fully their calling as caretakers.

vines worth a thousand silver shekels, there will be only briers and thorns" (NIV). One thousand speaks of the full measure of what God requires from His investment. Our Lord has given us all we need to bring forth fruit. He has given us talents, spiritual gifts, and graces, and He has anointed us to minister in His vineyard. We must till the soil, cultivate it, and tend it until it reaches full maturity.

Jesus receives His thousand shekels of silver every time a life comes into the maturity seen in the maiden in the Song of Songs. The Shulamite can now say to the King, "See, here are Your thousand shekels of silver (redemption), the mature ones that are fruit-bearing vines in Your kingdom. Your divine life now flows in them, as it does in me. We are branches united in love to You, the vine of heaven." Listen to her words:

> **But as for my own vineyard of love,**
> **I give it all to you forever.**
> **And I will give double honor to those who serve my beloved**
> **and have watched over my soul. (8:12)**

"But as for my own vineyard of love, I give it all to you forever." Her own life is fully given to Him as His life of fruitfulness and virtue shines in her. Her vine is worth a thousand shekels of silver, and now she gives Jesus all He expects from her. His work is complete; she is bearing His image. In 1:6 she was made a keeper of vineyards though she neglected her own—now her own vineyard is full and mature, bearing magnificent fruit. God wanted this fruit in Eden, and now He tastes it in her.

"And I will give double honor to those who serve my Beloved and have watched over my soul." This double portion comes to the faithful elders who are worthy of their reward (1 Tim. 5:17). Many are those who helped her in her journey, those who had gone on before her. They are to receive this portion of two hundred (fruit, not shekels). The Lord will not forget those who have labored in His name (Heb. 6:10).

My beloved, one with me in my garden,
how marvelous that my friends, the brides-to-be,
now hear your voice and song.
Let me now hear it again. (8:13)

What a beautiful journey into God's heart of love. His mighty love has carried her through. From a life of darkness under the sun to a life of fullness and glorious fruitfulness, this is the power of His grace. It has worked in her to do His good pleasure (Phil. 2:13). Have you seen yourself in this sacred journey? Can you see what the King longs to do in you? Wherever you are on this journey, there is a burning fire blazing before you. It is the fire of love that will not let you go. It's no wonder it has left a song in your heart that you want the world to hear. The Shulamite beckons everyone to hear this song and come into the garden of His fruitfulness to be forever changed into His likeness.

We've come to the end our journey together as we witness the closing exchange of love between the maiden and the King. It is a sacred ending, the happiest of all endings. Content forever, the King and His bride will become the eternal city of love and dwell together as one.

The King has a final desire filling His heart: "Let Me hear your voice again." He longs to hear her voice, the song of her heart, her intercession for His coming. How sweet is your voice to the Lord as well. It thrills His heart to hear you pray, to speak, and to sing to and with Him. Your voice is a source of pleasure to the King. The Lord wants to continually hear your voice in four different ways: First, in *worship* as He forever wants to hear us declare our love to Him. Second, in *intercession* as we join Jesus who makes intercession forever (Heb. 7:25). Third, in *teaching* as we speak the Word to one another (Matt. 28:19–20; Col. 1:28). And fourth, in *evangelism* as we share the gospel to unbelievers. The enemy wants to silence our voice; Jesus longs to hear our voice.

If the Shulamite's voice was sweet to Him in her immaturity

(2:14), how much more sweet is it to Him now that her devotion is complete as His bridal partner? Lifting our voices to Him in worship, adoration, and prayer ministers to His heart. To pray is to satisfy His longings. Does this give you a desire to pray? May our voices be ever sweet to Him! May our teaching and feeding of others be a sweet sound in His ears.

The King commissions the bride to intercede and remain faithful to her Bridegroom until He returns to take her to an eternal honeymoon. And she can be found in the garden as she diligently labors for Him. In the various aspects of equipping and tending the vineyard, she has remained loyal to Him. She has made the garden her dwelling. She has purposed to have a continued involvement in the body. The King's title of her is one of great respect and honor—she is occupied with His concerns. Truly, He is her garden.

The *"brides-to-be"* are those who have received from her ministry. They're "friends" who will one day become Shulamites themselves. They too are listening to the voice, the song of the bride, learning holy passion for their Beloved.

And His final encouragement to her is this: "My precious darling, in all your labors and ministry to others, let Me hear your voice. Lift up your song to Me. As you release the beautiful love song of your heart to Me, others will hear it and will stop to listen. Don't neglect the place of worship, intercession, and intimate prayer. This is My longing—to hear your voice! Never let busyness, offense, tensions, and pressures drown out your daily devotion to minister to My heart. Let nothing stop your sweet voice from singing your sweet song of love to Me."

Every time you whisper, "I love You, Lord," you are bringing the most precious sound to His ears. Let your cry for revival, your night and day intercession, be a continual love song to the Son of God. As you sing your song of love to Him, you will minister His love to others and watch revival come to you and to those you minister to.

Let's listen one more time to the King and His beloved bride singing their final chorus over one another. The song ends with their hearts pouring out their affirmation over each other. Now we must hear their parting sighs as they long to be together forever. Let's listen to the divine duet of the Bridegroom and the bride as they join their voices as one:

Arise, my darling!
Come quickly, my beloved.
Come and be the graceful gazelle with me.
Come be like a dancing deer with me.
We will dance in the high place of the sky,
yes, on the mountains of fragrant spice.
Forever we shall be united as one! (8:14)

The bride loves this King and the King loves her. She not only enthralls Him, but she understands Him now. And her spirit erupts with a cry from her inner being as her voice cries out in unison with His. They are united in urgency and a desperate longing in their hearts to call forward the brides-to-be, like the groaning of creation longing for the manifestations of the sons and daughters of God.

To be with Him is her victory, her dream come true. Fervent love has made her one with her beloved Bridegroom-King, a conqueror over every difficulty. So now they call out to each other, *"Come and be the graceful gazelle with me. Come be like a dancing deer with me. We will dance in the high place of the sky, yes, on the mountains of fragrant spice."* Forever they will rejoice and dance, dancing in the highest realms of glory, rejoicing over their glorious union together. Jesus is the Lord of the dance as He ever so skillfully leads us into the most beautiful dance of all time. We dance the dance of all dances as we sing the song of all songs! *"Forever we shall be united as one!"* The bride has finally made it into her full inheritance. Now that's really something to sing about. Lift up your voice and rejoice today.

And so the Song of Songs ends as it begins. This time, the bride is leaping and running with Him. Her prayer has been answered. He drew her, and now she runs after Him. She is echoing the very words He once spoke to draw her to the mountains. Now her desire is fulfilled in Him as they steal away together and run, dancing together upon the mountaintops.

She has said "I do" to the King. What divine partners they make. Wooed and pursued. Spinning, twirling, skipping together. It is a marriage made in heaven. They are bride and Bridegroom forever, like gazelles leaping in resurrection power. Their love is as innocent as a spring morning, pure as a mountain spring. What joy they find together on the mountains of fragrant spice. Arm in arm they join together in the ancient dance before the Ancient of Days.

The Shulamite says, "Come away and skip again, O mighty King. Dance in the gladness of Your heart. Leap over the mountains as You did when You swept my heart away!" Just married! The *"mountains of fragrant spice"* are peaks of pleasure that we will experience together. Unspeakable happiness awaits us forever. Forever! Dancing together in unbroken communion in the high places of the sky, we too will one day skip with Him, never to be separated again. "I love You, my King! You are my Lover-Friend! I will never let You go! Never."

Forever we shall be united as one! (8:14)

MORE FROM BRIAN & CANDICE SIMMONS

Be sure to visit

www.stairwayministries.org

for the latest release of The Passion Translation.

And go to

www.passiontranslation.com

for the updates of the new translation of the Bible: The Passion
Translation, which includes the translation of the
Song of Songs, Divine Romance.

You may contact Brian or Candice Simmons by emailing

brian@passiontranslation.com

Connect with Brian and The Passion Translation
on social media:

Facebook.com/passiontranslation
Twitter.com @tPtBible
Instagram.com/passiontranslation

Notes

Notes

Notes

Notes

Notes

Notes

www.thepassiontranslation.com